The world is full of
obvious things which nobody
by any chance ever observes.

—Sherlock Holmes

The Hound of the Baskervilles by Arthur Conan Doyle

HOW TO SEE WHAT OTHERS MISS NON-OBVIOUS THINKING

"The non-obvious way fuels breakthrough thinking!"

—**TONY ROBBINS**, #1 *NY Times* Bestselling Author

"In an age of echo chambers and confirmation bias, this book will open your eyes, uncork your brain, and inspire you to think bigger."

—**DANIEL H. PINK**, #1 *NY Times* Bestselling Author of *Drive*, *A Whole New Mind*, and *The Power of Regret*

"Any big leaps or innovations in society come from non-obvious thinking. This is a must-read for anyone looking to make these types of leaps for themselves or society."

—**SAL KHAN**, Founder & CEO of Khan Academy

"Don't settle for being Captain Obvious! If you have ever wondered how to see, create, and think better and differently, *Non-Obvious Thinking* is the motivation and handbook you've been looking for. And it's as fun to read as it is actionable!"

—**DOLLY CHUGH**, NYU Stern Professor & Bestselling Author

"A delightful guide to questioning old assumptions and seeing new possibilities."

ADAM GRANT, #1 *NY Times* Bestselling Author of *Think Again* and *Hidden Potential*

"This is an important book. I could start that way—and mean it. But I won't. How about, 'This book is a source of cover-to-cover joy. I had fun reading it.' I had tried five new-to-me things by page 25. 'Joy' and 'fun' are the words I choose to hang this endorsement on. It is a wonderful book. Play with it, put it down a hundred times, and try something. Bravo!"

—**TOM PETERS**, #1 Global Bestselling Coauthor of *In Search of Excellence*

"It's been said that the obvious isn't obvious until someone points it out to you, which often hinders our ability to solve complex problems and unlock opportunity. Fortunately, Rohit and Ben provide a means for us to hack our biology and see what's in plain sight."

—**DR. MARCUS COLLINS**, Author of *For the Culture*

"I have attended several of Ben duPont's Non-Obvious dinners. I have experienced the enjoyment of bringing some naturally curious individuals together for conversation to explore non-obvious ways of thinking about the world ahead. Discover the possibilities of Non-Obvious thinking."

—**JOHN SCULLEY**, Entrepreneur and former CEO of Apple

NON-OBVIOUS THINKING

ROHIT BHARGAVA AND BEN DUPONT

IDEAPRESS
PUBLISHING

WASHINGTON, DC

IDEAPRESS
PUBLISHING

Ideapress Publishing | www.ideapresspublishing.com

All trademarks are the property of their respective companies.

Cover Design: Faceout Studio, Elisha Zepeda
Illustrations: Scott Ward
Interior Design: Jessica Angerstein

Cataloging-in-Publication Data is on file with the Library of Congress.

Hardcover ISBN: 978-1-64687-161-2

Special Sales
Ideapress books are available at a special discount for bulk purchases for sales promotions and premiums, or for use in corporate training programs. Special editions, including personalized covers, custom forewords, corporate imprints, and bonus content are also available.

1 2 3 4 5 6 7 8 9 10

NON-
OBVIOUS
THINKING

Sift /*sift*/ verb

Examine (something) thoroughly to isolate
that which is most important or useful.

NON - OBVIOUS THINKING

BOOK STORYBOARD

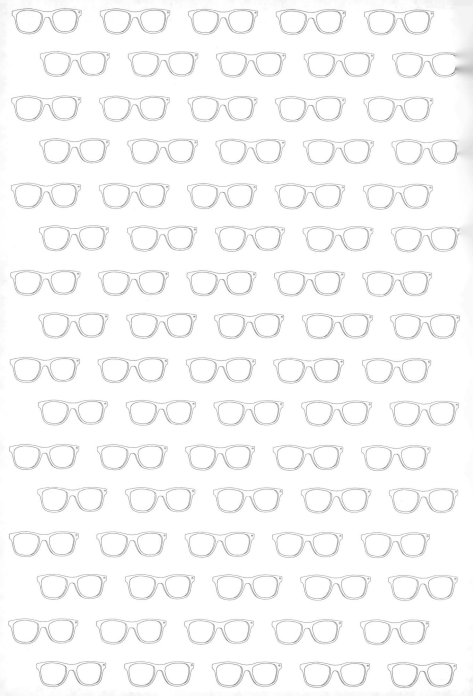

Introduction

On a Sunday afternoon in Mexico City, eighty thousand spectators gathered in the city's largest stadium to accidentally witness history. It was the last day of competition in the 1968 Summer Olympics, and the crowd was about to watch the final efforts of the remaining competitors in the high jump.

Two of the three athletes clearly belonged there.

Russian legend Valeriy Brumel was the reigning Olympic champion and favorite to win. Running in a close second was American Ed Caruthers, a world-class athlete who had also been drafted into the NFL. The third and most unlikely finalist was a tall, gangly engineering student named Dick Fosbury, who had showed up that morning for the biggest competition of his life wearing two mismatched shoes.

Despite his awkward appearance, he was the main attraction. The reason was his unusual technique.

Until then, the traditional way to high jump was by using the scissors technique, which involved getting the first leg over the bar, followed by the other. Fosbury, however, had a different approach. His method involved running up to the bar, turning backward, and propelling himself over while his body faced the sky. They called it the "Fosbury Flop."

That day, Fosbury cleared 2.24 meters, setting an Olympic record—enough to win the gold medal. Since that afternoon more than five decades ago, nearly every medalist in the high jump event has used Fosbury's flop technique. Fosbury won by turning his back on the traditional method and inventing a new way to compete.

The science fiction film *Ready Player One* takes place in a world where people immerse themselves in a virtual universe to escape the harsh reality of life on a ravaged Earth. Against this backdrop, eccentric genius James Halliday announces a video game contest to find an heir to his trillion-dollar fortune.

Wade Watts is among the many players trying to solve this virtual treasure hunt, beginning with its first task: a seemingly unwinnable car race. For years, no one has come close to completing the challenge. But inspiration  strikes our main hero. As the race starts, Wade stalls his car and immediately starts driving in reverse. That unexpected choice unlocks a new path, allowing him to avoid obstacles the others face and win the race.

Wade conquers that first quest by shifting his perspective and unlocking a road that had been invisible until that moment.

———————

Joy Buolamwini had to wear a white mask to be seen. As an MIT graduate student in computer science working to train social robots on facial recognition, she realized that her dark skin wasn't recognized by the generic software used by most of these robots. The problem was algorithmic bias built into facial recognition systems, which she described as the "coded gaze."

Buolamwini's solution was to start a movement for more inclusive technology. Her organization, the Algorithmic Justice League, has become a gathering point where technologists and citizens can report experiences of algorithmic bias.

In recognition of her impact, Buolamwini has been named one of the world's Most Creative People. Her work has influenced new global legislation, inspired the mission of ethics groups within corporations, and was chronicled in the award-winning Netflix documentary *Coded Bias*.

On the surface, an unexpected Olympic champion, a fictional teenage video gamer, and an invisible computer scientist don't seem to have much in common. Yet each managed to do one of the most challenging things anyone can do: find a non-obvious solution that others had missed.

Seeing What Others Don't

Detective stories typically feature a hero solving a case by piecing together a theory from many small observations that only they have made. Like the unaware secondary characters in a good mystery story, we can also get distracted by big things and fail to notice minor details that seem insignificant at first—but turn out to be the clues that ultimately help solve the case.

Fosbury noticed that when his sport moved to using foam mats as landing pads in the high jump event, it offered a chance for athletes to land safely in ways they couldn't before. His observation led him to develop his famous flop technique … and win the gold medal.

The character Wade Watts solved the key to the virtual car race using his knowledge of James Halliday's life. He remembered reading a small detail in Halliday's virtual diary that proved to be the clue to understanding him and making the winning choice to find a different path.

Joy Buolamwini took up the study of algorithmic bias after she experienced the frustration of being ignored by facial recognition software due to the color of her skin while working with robots in a lab. Realizing the real-life consequences of that experience prompted her to do something about it.

These are not examples of geniuses or once-in-a-lifetime talents. Instead, they are both real and imagined stories of people who taught themselves to pay attention to the details overlooked by everyone else. Learning to do this starts with observation, but it takes more than just noticing the details around you.

> The goal of this book is to teach you how to overcome blind spots and become a more original thinker.

We call this "non-obvious thinking." And the search for *how* to do it has shaped both of our professional lives.

Seeking the Non-Obvious

For Rohit, seeking non-obvious ideas started when he worked at one of the world's biggest ad agencies. He was part of an unusual task force working to dream up new ways to apply behavioral science to create more persuasive marketing.

This deep work studying human behavior and influence led Rohit to write the "Non-Obvious Trend Report" the following year. The report went viral, reaching more than two hundred thousand professionals, and became the springboard for Rohit's bestselling series of annual Non-Obvious books about predicting trends that would run for ten years, reaching more than a million readers.

While Rohit was exploring non-obvious ideas through his research and books, Ben was building a deeply engaged community around non-obvious thinking too. For the past twenty years, his annual Non-Obvious Dinner event has brought together a mix of US senators, CEOs, and Nobel Prize laureates alongside entrepreneurs, musicians, and high school students to imagine a better future.

{ Often the best ideas come from unexpected voices, the non-experts who bring an outsider's perspective. }

At every dinner, participants are challenged to share their most "non-obvious" ideas for changing the world. Each table picks their favorite, and the whole room then decides on the most significant idea of the evening. Some of the winning non-obvious ideas over the past decade have included shifting higher education to a three-year on-campus experience, using "digital exhaust" data to cure cancer, and solving the dilemma of who will take over family businesses when kids leave or seek a different life—the so-called rising "succession crisis"—among small-town businesses.

Whether hosting an unconventional gathering or interviewing researchers on the cutting edge of new technology, our work has individually offered each of us an intimate look at how fascinating minds work. Over the years, we both became obsessed with cataloging what we've learned about how some of the world's smartest and most creative people engage in non-obvious thinking. What mindsets and habits allow them to do what they do? What do they know that others don't? And, more importantly, can anyone learn to think and see the way they do with some training and practice?

This obsession brought us together to write this book because we believe that anyone can become a non-obvious thinker.

The SIFT Framework

Most bakers know that one of the secrets to making light airy cakes is sifting your dry ingredients. When you sift flour, for example, you eliminate lumps and incorporate air while removing impurities. The benefits of sifting offer a perfect metaphor to describe how you can start to think in more non-obvious ways too. Aside from baking, the word *sift* has another meaning: to isolate that which is most valuable.

It is this secondary meaning that led us to use the word as a memorable acronym for the method we will teach you in this book. Our goal is to help *you* become a non-obvious thinker. This starts with using the SIFT method:

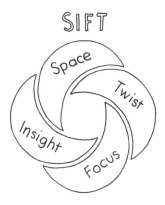

{ Before you can see what others miss, you must develop the mental flexibility to be open to new ideas. }

This process starts with creating more *space*. Space is the warmup stretch that makes limber, non-obvious thinking possible. In Part I, you will read about proven techniques for creating space, from reinventing your breathing to unearthing your mental biases.

Once you have learned to create more space, in Part II you will learn to uncover *insights*. Insights go beyond describing the world as we see it on the surface and explain *why* it is the way it is. Discovering them usually starts by asking better questions.

After you get better at collecting insights, you will need to narrow your attention to the things that matter most. In Part III, you will learn techniques to help you *focus*. This includes new suggestions to block out the many distractions we all face and see other perspectives unlike your own. To help you do it, we will share techniques to discover patterns, avoid the paradox of choice, and use constraints to improve your thinking.

The final stage in the SIFT framework is what we like to call the *twist*. This is the moment when you challenge yourself to take your thinking even further. If your mental journey to this point was akin to a high jump, this would be the moment when you raise the bar just a little higher. When you do this, it is not just for your own benefit. The impact of opening your mind to see new perspectives and welcome uncommon thinking may matter much more than any of us realize.

Non-Obvious Thinkers Wanted

At a time when social media algorithms fuel deep polarization in our society, our culture is desperate for more non-obvious thinkers. Old solutions for new problems rarely work. We need people who see what others don't, ask questions, and push back against the obvious status quo—people who have the empathy to put themselves in other people's shoes without dismissing alternate perspectives as misguided.

{ The world needs more non-obvious thinkers. }

Non-obvious thinkers are the instigators who come up with bold, original ideas that propel *all* of us forward—and have the courage and determination to turn them into reality. They are the ones who change things for the better. And every country on Earth is hungry for more of them.

You can become one. This book will show you how.

PART ONE

Create Space

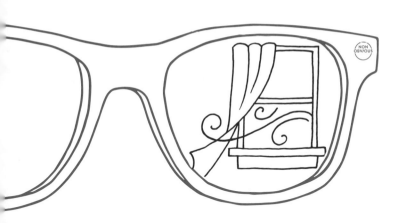

CREATE SPACE

In the closing days of 2019, just months before the COVID-19 pandemic hit, CNN published a list of the most influential books of the past decade. Among the novels and memoirs on the list, only one title promised to change your life—starting with teaching you how to fold your socks.

The Life-Changing Magic of Tidying Up, written by Japanese organizational expert Marie Kondo, became a worldwide sensation, selling millions of copies and even inspiring a Netflix series. The book and series showed people how to reduce the clutter in their lives by asking whether the things they own spark joy … and getting rid of those that don't. The main idea is to keep what you value most in your heart and discard what you don't.

The need to unclutter our lives extends far beyond our closets. Technology guarantees that we are never out of reach, yet we still feel disconnected. Entertainment is always on demand, and news is always "breaking" whether we demand it or not. All of it makes us feel as though we have less and less time for ourselves.

> { Carving out more time and reducing clutter does not guarantee more profound ideas or deeper fulfillment. }

This common obsession with time has driven advice on how to manage it into one of the largest categories of the self-help industry. Bestselling books inspire live seminars, reality shows, and popular podcasts about the upside of simplifying our lives by working a shorter week, quitting our day jobs, and even folding our socks more intentionally.

Underlying these suggestions and life hacks is the belief that having more time would naturally result in better productivity, greater happiness, and more groundbreaking thinking. Unfortunately, the recipe for innovation or happiness is rarely so easy.

Creating space goes beyond simply producing more time for contemplation. Sometimes it also involves creating the physical space to have new ideas. Or being more productive with the free time you do have so you can invest it in ways that can help you open your mind into unexplored directions and be more receptive to non-obvious insights.

Yes, having more time *can* help. But cultivating more mental agility to truly benefit from this additional space is the real cornerstone of non-obvious thinking, and it requires more than just reducing clutter or clearing your to-do list. In this section, you will learn proven techniques to create space, starting with something that you do every day but hardly ever think about.

CREATE SPACE

Start With Breathing

Ditch Your Prebuttals

Make Oasis Moments

Embrace Danger

Change Your Rituals

Allow Time Spaciousness

CREATE SPACE //

Start With Breathing

The *Iceman* doesn't feel cold—at least not like the rest of us.

Wim Hof is a Dutch extreme athlete who has climbed Mount Kilimanjaro in shorts, run a half marathon above the Arctic Circle barefoot, and set 18 Guinness World Records (so far). He has long believed that the secret to accomplishing his extraordinary feats is his self-taught ability to control an essential bodily function: how he breathes.

Even if you're not considering a new career in extreme sports, there's a valuable lesson in the Iceman's story. For an instinctual human function fundamental to life, surprising new science suggests we have much to learn about what good breathing truly means. Without proper breathing, our thinking can remain constrained and obvious. Shallow breathing can often lead to shallow thinking too.

> { Breathing may be something we do every day, but most of us have never learned how to do it "right." }

When science journalist James Nestor arrived in Kalamata, Greece, on assignment to document the world of free diving—a superhuman sport that involves diving hundreds of feet into the ocean on a single breath for minutes on end—he was surprised by the group of athletes competing that day.

Contrary to what you might assume, these extreme competitors were not particularly physically gifted or winners of any sort of genetic lottery awarding them above average lung capacity. Instead, as one free diver explained to Nestor, they had discovered that "there are as many ways to breathe as there are foods to eat."

Nestor reasoned that if this were true, there must be a better (and worse) way of breathing. He started investigating the research and quickly found that the way most of us breathe has become worse and worse over time.

Instead of taking longer and deeper breaths throughout the day, most of us *overbreathe* by taking shorter and shallower breaths than we should. The "perfect breath," as Nestor discovered, is inhaling for 5.5 seconds and exhaling for the same amount of time. His bestselling book *Breath* helped rekindle public awareness about the importance of good breathing.

The idea that you should focus on your breathing may strike you as a rather obvious place to start a book about non-obvious thinking. Yet when you start to pay attention to something so regularly overlooked, the side benefit is that you can also awaken a part of your mind that has otherwise become very good at accomplishing the mundane without requiring too much thinking.

Your daily habits and familiar routines represent a form of detail blindness. You don't notice the things around you because your mind tells you they are unimportant. But when you start paying attention to your breathing, you can break this pattern. Breathing with purpose helps you do everything else with purpose too, which makes it the ideal first step to create the space required for non-obvious thinking to happen.

HOW TO
Start With Breathing

Pretend Someone Is Watching

If you take a breathing class in-person (which we wholeheartedly recommend), there will probably be someone watching you at some point. Even on your own, though, it can be helpful to imagine you have an audience. Breathing is so automatic for each of us that inventing a scenario where you're being observed can help trick your brain into sticking with the new routine and keep you from taking shortcuts.

Set Breathing Reminders

You might not think you need reminders to do something your body does instinctually. But if you want to maintain better breathing habits, integrating reminders to breathe properly into your routine does make a difference. Set up phone alerts, leave reminder notes in strategic places, or even schedule time in your calendar for mindful breathing. The more intentionally you can retrain yourself, the more quickly you can make better breathing a habit.

CREATE SPACE

Start With Breathing

Ditch Your Prebuttals

Make Oasis Moments

Embrace Danger

Change Your Rituals

Allow Time Spaciousness

CREATE SPACE //

Ditch Your Prebuttals

The most toxic tool in modern politics and business is undoubtedly the prebuttal.

If a rebuttal is, at its best, a thoughtful response refuting an argument someone makes, then a prebuttal is its far less intelligent cousin. A prebuttal is a counterargument to what someone might say *before* they ever say it. It is the equivalent of shouting your disagreement with an unspoken idea, effectively shutting down any chance for genuine dialogue. Prebuttals declare to the world that instead of choosing to listen and think, those who employ them believe that their perspective is the only one that matters.

In the buildup to political debates and elections, news media routinely offers a platform to people who expertly offer up one prebuttal after another. Their hollow statements fuel division, flame controversy, and induce rage instead of fostering substantive discussions.

{ Prebuttals are a lazy coping mechanism that can lead anyone toward a more narrow-minded perspective. }

Fortunately, unless you're actually working on a political campaign, most of us don't operate in communities or workplaces where prebuttals are commonplace. Yet the mindset that motivates them often shows up in our daily lives in more ordinary ways.

Avoiding reconnecting with an old high-school classmate because you recall a slight from years ago is a form of prebuttal. Judging a co-worker as incompetent based on a single thoughtless comment or mistake from the past is a form of prebuttal. Deciding that you will hate something *before* trying it is a form of self-directed prebuttal.

When you prebuttle, you do the opposite of creating the space needed to consider new people, ideas, or viewpoints. You stunt your growth as a person. Human interactions aren't meant to be battlegrounds where you argue until you win. They can be opportunities to understand and see things you might have otherwise missed ... if you let them.

To avoid becoming a "prebuttaler," start with a conscious choice not to engage in a conversation or situation with a dismissive attitude. Keep yourself from making snap judgments in the moment and take more time to be thoughtful. The old saying that there are no bad ideas isn't entirely accurate—there have always been bad ideas. But in real time, discerning between good and bad ideas is difficult. Reserve your criticism, listen to new perspectives, and allow some time to pass before forming an opinion.

Creating space starts with listening rather than anticipating disagreements. Learning to ditch your prebuttals can help you do that.

HOW TO
Ditch Your Prebuttals

Ask Yourself Why

Do you believe that breaking a mirror or seeing a black cat will bring bad luck? Do some questions bother you more than others? What makes something a "pet peeve" of yours, and how do you react when someone does it? Do you have a belief that you know is illogical, but you choose to retain it anyway? These can be difficult questions to ask yourself. When you do, however, it can lead to the sort of self-awareness that can help you silence your inner prebuttaler.

See Through Prebuttalers

Political pundits are easy to spot, but people outside of politics who are similarly biased can blend in far more easily. Sometimes they might excuse their actions by suggesting that they are just playing a "devil's advocate" or try to use humor to disguise their cynicism. To see them, look for telltale signs of prebuttalers such as persistent negativity and a need to dominate every conversation. The faster you can identify them, the more prepared you can be to maintain your skepticism and seek out more balanced perspectives instead.

CREATE SPACE

Start With Breathing

Ditch Your Prebuttals

Make Oasis Moments

Embrace Danger

Change Your Rituals

Allow Time Spaciousness

CREATE SPACE //

Make Oasis Moments

It is 9:08 a.m. in the lobby of a hotel in the middle of Austin, Texas. More than two hundred attendees of the South by Southwest (SXSW) annual conference are standing shoulder to shoulder in anticipation of what is about to happen. In sixty seconds, it is going to get loud. Really loud.

The flash mob of conversations that ensue are part of the Non-Obvious 7-Minute Meetup, a quirky gathering our team envisioned to solve the problem of disconnection.

SXSW brings together a diverse blend of musicians, filmmakers, large brands, and startup founders for ten exhilarating days of performances, knowledge sharing, intense networking, and collaboration. With hundreds of sessions, the conference is ordered chaos. It takes over large and small venues across the city and fills every hour of the day. It's common for first-time attendees and longtime participants to feel isolated and overwhelmed.

The Non-Obvious 7-Minute Meetup was created to offer a moment for everyone to slow down and feel a tiny sense of belonging amidst the hustle. Those who joined were encouraged to make personal connections in a sea of faces, starting with sharing something non-obvious about themselves with a stranger.

> { An oasis moment offers refuge from the usual noise and chaos of the everyday, allowing for reflection and open-mindedness. }

Over the years, these simple meetups have sparked business partnerships, client engagements, and even led to a few romantic relationships. We have since recreated this meetup at dozens of other live events around the world to provoke more authentic conversations.

What makes these short gatherings so impactful?

They offer a time-constrained chance to reset akin to half-time during a soccer game. Taking a short break from a chaotic situation, even just for a few minutes, can help prevent over-stimulation in the wrong moment. In her popular book *Quiet*, author Susan Cain explains that one key difference between introverts and extroverts is the amount of stimulation they deem comfortable. While each of us has different ideal levels of stimulation, we all reach a point when we must regroup and quiet ourselves to recharge.

The luxury of someone else orchestrating such a moment of calm for you is rare. But you can—and should—create moments like this for yourself. When you feel overwhelmed, it is impossible to engage fully with what's happening around you. That makes it more likely you will fail to notice important details, unintentionally minimize someone's perspective, or miss the chance to encounter and digest new ideas.

Finding "oasis moments" where you can slow down and reflect for a few minutes is the ideal way to create space in unusually crowded or busy moments. The space you make could be the starting point for seeing new things you never would have noticed or connecting with people you might not have otherwise met.

HOW TO
Make Oasis Moments

Pick a Set Time

Since they are meant to offer breaks from a busy, chaotic, or noisy time, oasis moments can be challenging to squeeze into the moments when we need them the most. To make it easier, try to anticipate which upcoming situations or events might be the most overstimulating for you. Then, prioritize taking a moment apart from the bustle by picking a set time to make it happen—even if the moment only lasts for seven minutes!

Anchor Your Attention

You don't need total silence or even physical isolation to create oasis moments. One way to do this is by selectively anchoring your attention by focusing on a color, shape, smell, or any other minor detail around you. What are all the blue things around you? Train your eye on anything that's round. Reducing your gaze in this way is an easy little trick you can use to give yourself a mental break and create space in a unique way.

Start With Breathing

Ditch Your Prebuttals

Make Oasis Moments

Embrace Danger

Change Your Rituals

Allow Time Spaciousness

CREATE SPACE //

Embrace Danger

The Land, a playground on the outskirts of Wrexham in North Wales, is famous for its unconventional rules—or lack of them. Here, children set fires and play with sharp objects. In fact, this sort of play is encouraged.

The unusual park first captured the public eye through a documentary showing children playing with hammers and saws and doing all sorts of dangerous activities—with minimal adult supervision. Unlike traditional playgrounds where children get bored quickly, this "space full of possibilities," as its tagline boasted, was wildly popular with children of all genders because of how different it was from all the others.

Curiously, there were no more reported injuries at The Land than at other playgrounds. Researchers came up with an interesting theory to explain this paradox: the dangers of the park might be motivating children to play more carefully, rely on one another, and be more aware of their surroundings. If this theory were true, researchers began to ponder an even bigger question: What if the very features of most playgrounds meant to protect kids, such as rubber turf, unnecessarily insulated them from learning how to protect themselves in the real world?

> Embrace danger and invite friction into your life to heighten your awareness and build resilience.

We might pose a similar question about many aspects of our adult lives, too. Aggressive corporate email spam filters prevent messages from unfamiliar sources. Warning labels remind us not to use items as personal flotation devices in an emergency— even if they actually float. Meanwhile, one-button solutions for cooking or parking cocoon us from inconvenience.

When we bubble-wrap our world to make it ultra-safe or super-easy (or both), we risk losing the ability to learn from the mistakes we never make. Proving this point, multiple studies have shown that habitual use of GPS has negatively affected our spatial memory. In other words, Google Maps is killing our sense of direction (and, perhaps, our willingness to pursue unknown paths). It's easy to cruise through life absentmindedly when everything around you is safe and easy.

Embracing opportunities to take risks and make mistakes, on the other hand, opens you to push your own mental and physical boundaries. When we are in this heightened state of awareness from a hazardous situation, we are more likely to see things we otherwise would have ignored.

Taking more chances is not about recklessly careening ourselves down the equivalent of an icy road without a seat belt. Rather, it is about creating more space for experimentation and saying yes to more unfamiliar experiences.

Whether maplessly navigating a new city or trying an extreme sport, allowing more danger and friction into your life can be an effective way to create the mental space you need to welcome new ideas.

HOW TO
Embrace Danger

Turn Off the Guides

Taking risks can be as simple as deactivating the map in your smartphone and navigating without assistance. It might also include cooking without a recipe or building furniture without instructions. Trying to speak a new language amidst a  group of native speakers can also feel risky. Removing the usual guides or rules for any situation can heighten your awareness of what's happening around you and create space for new experiences.

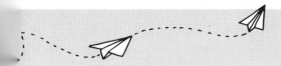

Switch It Up

The older we get, the more we stick to safe bets—what we know how to do already. Making bold changes can be an ideal starting point to break out of this mindset. Switch from skiing to snowboarding.  Take a standup comedy class. Don't go on vacation to the same destination twice. Embracing the unfamiliar and new can help your mind peel back a layer of self-protection and create more space for new ways of thinking and seeing.

CREATE SPACE

Start With Breathing

Ditch Your Prebuttals

Make Oasis Moments

Embrace Danger

Change Your Rituals

Allow Time Spaciousness

Change Your Rituals

In medieval Europe, beer was considered the breakfast of champions thanks to its high caloric value. The alcohol content probably helped its popularity too.

Across parts of Southeast Asia, a traditional Ayurvedic morning routine might consist of a sequence of mindful self-care actions that includes scraping your tongue and washing your eyes.

Modern self-help experts suggest positive daily habits like starting every day by writing down a list of priorities, having a healthy breakfast, and absolutely, most definitely *never* checking your phone from bed right when you wake up.

What you do first in the morning matters—which is why everyone seems to have an opinion about it. Although experts may offer different advice about morning rituals, they seem to align on one suggestion: For any of these daily habits to work, you must stick to them. Consistency is key.

Or is it?

> To avoid getting stuck in a mental rut, try something different in the first moments of your day.

Rituals are often presented as going hand in hand with perseverance and dedication. While morning rituals do have the potential to evolve into positive habits, they can also get us into a mental rut. As they harden into rigid routines, they can have the effect of setting our brains on autopilot. And when we are in this sort of instinctual mode, we stop thinking. If what we do first in the morning matters, starting every day in the same way can make non-obvious thinking much harder.

Here's an alternative way to think about starting your day: What if you treated your morning rituals as a series of experiments? For a week, try drinking chai instead of coffee. Or charge your phone in a different location out of reach from where you sleep. Or choose one non-weekend day a week to wake up much earlier (or much later) than usual.

Renowned chef and father of molecular gastronomy Ferran Adrià was once asked during an interview for *TIME* magazine to share his "go-to breakfast." He responded by sharing his non-obvious habit of eating a different fruit every morning for a month. It's a small example of how one of the most creative chefs in the world trains his mind for possibilities by making one simple change to his morning routine.

By injecting some novelty into the first moments of your day, you can achieve the same effect. Instead of starting this morning in automatic mode, mindlessly craving that first cup of coffee, you can send a powerful signal to your mind that this is a day to be engaged and receptive to new perspectives and ideas.

HOW TO
Change Your Rituals

Reverse Your Routines

Spend a week writing down all the things (big and small) that you do in the first hour of every day. Then change the order that you do them and add at least one new ritual. If you

typically shower before making breakfast, try reversing those two activities and doing something unusual, such as taking time to read the "poem of the day" from the *Poetry* magazine website. Forcing yourself to break patterns of activity while simultaneously trying something new can encourage the brain to make space for new ideas too.

Apply the Five-Second Rule

Sometimes, we are reluctant to shift routines because what we already do feels so comfortable. If you are having difficulty making changes, consider self-help guru Mel Robbins's advice:

Before starting a new ritual, do a simple countdown—5, 4, 3, 2 ... 1. And then try the change without any further hesitation. This five-second exercise can help you take that difficult first step toward a new outlook on your day.

CREATE SPACE

Start With Breathing

Ditch Your Prebuttals

Make Oasis Moments

Embrace Danger

Change Your Rituals

Allow Time Spaciousness

CREATE SPACE //

Allow Time Spaciousness

Right about the time when one of the biggest movie directors in the world was supposed to begin shooting a blockbuster sequel to the top-grossing film of all time, he was sitting inside a tiny submarine instead, on a quest to complete the first solo dive to the Mariana Trench, the deepest point in the world's oceans.

It would be another four years before James Cameron would set foot on a set to start production on the film ... which should hardly have been a surprise because the first installment in his Avatar movie series took nearly a dozen years to complete. Of course, if anyone had earned the right to get away with working with this sort of timeline, it was Cameron.

He is the only director with three films grossing $2 billion or more at the box office: *Titanic* in 1997, *Avatar* in 2009, and *Avatar 2: The Way of Water* in 2022. When complete, the Avatar saga will have taken more than 30 years of his life and could earn well over $10 billion. Clearly, James Cameron is not in a rush.

Most of us don't enjoy the same sort of clout that a famous Hollywood director can wield to get away with such extended schedules, but we can still learn a few lessons from his example. Despite the external pressures to deliver faster, Cameron spent four years perfecting the scripts for all five planned films before shooting a single scene of the second film.

Imagine you could employ this sort of thinking for the biggest things in your life.

Perhaps the most widely read self-help book ever written, Dale Carnegie's *How to Win Friends and Influence People*, only happened after a literary agent finally convinced a reluctant Carnegie to publish the book after years of persistence. By the time the book came out in 1936, Carnegie had been teaching his signature course on public speaking and human relations for 24 years. When it debuted, it was an instant hit, going on to sell more than 30 million copies worldwide and becoming one of the bestselling books of all time.

{ Practicing time spaciousness can help you avoid feeling constantly hurried or pressured by time constraints. }

Author Jane McGonigal teaches people how to have more urgent optimism about the future and describes *time spaciousness* as "the relaxing and empowering feeling that we have enough time to do what really matters."

Allowing for more time spaciousness, like being more patient, can be challenging because it demands that we ignore some of the pressure the world puts on our shoulders. Giving yourself more time starts with the mental permission to slow down without feeling that any self-imposed pause is a failure.

That invisible clock constantly urging us to achieve personal and professional success as quickly as possible also pushes us to speed through our thinking, often resulting in status quo, obvious thinking. To enable your best ideas to simmer, and unexpected connections to surface, start by silencing this clock. When you allow more time for thoughtfulness, you can help create space for your best thinking to shine.

HOW TO
Allow Time Spaciousness

Reject an Unnecessary Deadline Mindset

Learn to distinguish between externally imposed inflexible deadlines (like college application due dates) and self-imposed arbitrary ones (like owning a house by age 30). The more you relinquish these self-created time constraints, the more space you can create for new thinking and ideas. Ironically, when you do this, the space you create can empower you to take concrete steps toward hitting that arbitrary deadline because you are not so singularly focused on chasing it.

Be a Traveler, Not a Tourist

Organized travel tours are excellent at fitting many itinerary stops into an short window of time. Unfortunately, they can also make it harder to truly experience the magic of a destination. Spending a rushed 25 minutes taking the ferry past the Sydney Opera House is different from spending an afternoon sitting outside enjoying a glass of wine at a harbor bar and witnessing two passing strangers getting engaged just in front of the iconic building. These are the things that happen when you take your time with new experiences. Be a traveler, not a tourist.

PART TWO

Uncover Insights

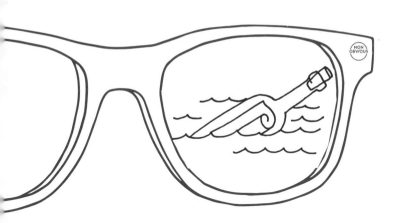

OVERVIEW //
UNCOVER INSIGHTS

A forensic sketch artist sits in a sparse warehouse in front of his drafting board. One by one, women are invited to sit near him behind a curtain. They cannot see him, and he can't see them.

The artist asks each woman to describe herself—starting with her nose, then chin, forehead, and eyes. Guided solely by their words, he draws their faces. Following each session, a different woman enters the room and is asked to describe the person who had come before her. The artist makes a second sketch of the same face, this time guided only by the stranger's description.

Finally, both sketches are hung side by side in rows across the warehouse. Slowly, the women are brought in to see the results of the experiment. The difference between the two portraits is striking. The sketches drawn from

self-descriptions show faces that are meaner, sadder, and less friendly than those based on strangers' descriptions.

{ An insight is a surprising truth that explains why things are the way they are. }

The juxtaposition reveals that many people judge themselves far more harshly than the world sees them. The *insight* of this experiment, part of Dove skincare's celebrated Real Beauty ad campaign, is summarized in its empowering tagline: "You are more beautiful than you think."

Turning observations into insights—such as seeing how easy it can be to focus on our flaws instead of what makes us beautiful—is a skill that all of us can learn. It is also fundamental to non-obvious thinking.

Often, insights come from deep listening, research, or analysis. Occasionally they get illustrated in cleverly conceived and effective advertising stunts. But the common starting point for insights is observation.

Uncovering an insight can afford a new way to understand behaviors, habits, and perspectives. In this section, you'll learn techniques to help you make and explore your own interesting observations and transform them into insights, starting with a better technique for listening that will evolve the way you approach any conversation.

ING: HOW TO SEE WHAT OTHERS MISS NON-OBVIOUS THINKING: HOW TO SEE WHAT OTHERS MISS NON-OBVIOUS THINKING
E WHAT OTHERS MISS NON-OBVIOUS THINKING: HOW TO SEE WHAT OTHERS MISS NON-OBVIOUS THINKING: HOW TO SEE
RS MISS NON-OBVIOUS THINKING: HOW TO SEE WHAT OTHERS MISS NON-OBVIOUS THINKING: HOW TO SEE WHAT OTHER
OBVIOUS THINKING: HOW TO SEE WHAT OTHERS MISS NON-OBVIOUS THINKING: HOW TO SEE WHAT OTHERS MISS NON-OF
ING: HOW TO SEE WHAT OTHERS NO

Ask Story Questions

If you could take a master class in asking questions, Jacqui Banaszynski might be the ideal person to lead it. A Pulitzer Prize–winning journalist and chair of the journalism department at the University of Missouri, Banaszynski has inspired aspiring journalists for decades with her methods.

One of the many techniques she teaches students is avoiding pre-scripted interview questions. Instead, she suggests a dynamic, circular technique that involves crafting each subsequent question of an interview based on the answer received to the previous question. The goal of this approach is to shift the focus away from looking for answers to eliciting stories instead.

When most of us are faced with the task of interviewing someone—perhaps for a job opening or to understand a new topic—we typically begin by writing a list of questions. When Rohit first started interviewing guests for his podcast, he did just that. After a dozen episodes, he realized that conversations with guests often followed a path that wasn't so easily dictated by a sequential list of questions. That was when he first learned about Banaszynski's method and decided to try it.

At first, it was challenging. It required quick thinking and a deeper concentration on the nuances of the answers his guests shared. Quickly, he also began to notice that the conversations were more genuine and free flowing. The feedback from listeners was more positive. The show itself became more authentic and personal.

The circular method elicits more candid responses because, as Banaszynski explains, "a storyteller question ... helps put people back into the movie of their own life; it puts them into a scene for a moment." To do this, one technique she recommends is inviting people to imagine how they might explain an idea to a classroom filled with children or to recall the senses rather than the emotions involved in a memory.

{ Asking questions that elicit stories rather than answers leads to more interesting observations. }

While most of us don't need to craft stories like investigative journalists, their methods for uncovering new truths can help all of us become better at gathering observations we otherwise may not be able to make. When we ask people "storytelling questions," we nudge them to tell us about their lives, histories, experiences, and perspectives. Their unexpected answers make for interesting stories and can lead to surprising insights along the way.

HOW TO
Ask Story Questions

Focus On the Afterthought

When people share stories, they often include tiny details that feel unimportant to them. These afterthoughts can be unexpected clues to an aspect of their story that they might never have given much conscious thought to. Ask why  they thought to mention it. The answer may lead them to consider their story in a different light and lead you to a new, unexpected insight too.

Practice With Question Trees

Every conversation is an oppor-
tunity to improve your question-
ing (and listening) skills. The
next time you engage someone
in a conversation, make a men-
tal commitment to ask them at least three questions in a row.
Try to relate each question to their previous answer. When this
becomes easy, increase the number to four. Then five. How
high can you go? Doing this will make you a better listener and
improve the depth and quality of your conversations too.

UNCOVER INSIGHTS

Ask Story Questions

Hone Your Nunchi

Get Your Hands Dirty

Spot Natural Wisdom

Find the Right Room

Step Into Others' Shoes

Hone Your Nunchi

Understanding what others think and feel without asking them directly is a familiar skill in Korean culture. Known as *nunchi* (pronounced noon-chee), this 5,000-year-old form of emotional intelligence is essential to navigating social pressures and sensitive topics. In Japan, there is a similar concept called *kuuki wo yomu* (pronounced koo-kee woh yoh-moo), which roughly translates to "reading the air" or being able to discern the unspoken meaning behind what people say and do.

Both philosophies operate on the principle that what is being said or done explicitly doesn't always reflect or match the actual meaning, deeper emotions, or intentions of others. The practice of reading body language is also based on this idea:

our physical actions reveal cues about our feelings that our words do not. Similarly, police interrogators have also learned to detect signs of lying by looking for subconscious bodily cues. Unusual rises or falls in vocal tones, non-congruent gestures (like nodding yes while saying no), and covering one's mouth while speaking are all telltale signs someone could be lying.

> { Being able to gauge the unspoken thoughts, feelings, and intentions of others opens a window into layers of meaning others often miss. }

In Western cultures, where directness is both expected and respected, learning to read the air and becoming better at reading body language can also supercharge your ability to uncover insights. It is like having access to the emotional subtitles of a situation, offering you an understanding and perspective that others who are less attuned will miss.

Some neurodiverse individuals do have difficulty seeing these social cues for reasons outside their control, but even those who struggle to read social cues can improve their social skills through direct instruction. This neurodiversity can also create perspectives that allow people to see or experience the world in entirely different and nuanced ways that most others are missing. This goes further than just recognizing that someone who is checking their watch or consistently looking away during a conversation may be distracted—though these are both good starting points.

Whether you grew up or currently live in a high-context culture where nunchi is constantly expected or not, you can improve your ability to read between the lines and understand the meanings of actions too. One ideal starting point? People-watching. Pay attention to how people interact in crowded places like airports or parks and in intimate places like quiet restaurants or coffee shops. When you do this frequently and become more adept at observing deeper details like how people relate to others while listening, the way they treat waiters and maintain eye contact, or whether they welcome newcomers into a conversation, you'll start to uncover an entire hidden layer of conversation.

Eventually, you may find it hard to ignore this added source of insight from other people's body language in every situation you find yourself in. It will seem impossible that once you were not able to pick up on the signals that you now find completely unmissable. That's the power of learning to hone your nunchi.

HOW TO
Hone Your Nunchi

Watch Something on Mute

The next time you watch a video, try turning down the volume— all the way down. When you can't hear what people say (and you don't use the captions), you force yourself to pay attention to nonverbal cues—and your brain fills in the rest. During the

1960 US presidential debate, Richard Nixon's nervous, shifty body language compared to the composure of John F. Kennedy was widely believed to be a turning point in the election. Nixon would go on to lose. Our bodies reveal many insights that our words often don't.

Broaden Your Attention

The details of the space you are in and the people around you can offer valuable background information ... if you notice them. When we enter a new situation too focused on a single objective or person, we can miss crucial contextual clues. For example, when two people are standing beside one another, does one seem to glance more frequently at the other? Noticing

this detail can help you figure out who's really in charge. When you train yourself to read the room, the nuances of any moment will move from the background into the

spotlight and you'll see the bigger picture.

UNCOVER INSIGHTS

Ask Story Questions

Hone Your Nunchi

Get Your Hands Dirty

Spot Natural Wisdom

Find the Right Room

Step Into Others' Shoes

Get Your Hands Dirty

Several years into his leadership role at Uber, CEO Dara Khosrowshahi sent out a company-wide meeting invite with an unusually blunt subject line: *Why we suck.*

The meeting had been prompted by Khosrowshahi's experience going undercover as a driver on the platform and getting to know his company's product from the perspective of a gig worker delivering food and giving people rides. It wasn't good.

The idea that experiencing a job firsthand is invaluable is also the driving force behind the long-running reality television show *Undercover Boss.* For eleven seasons, it chronicled upper-management leaders taking entry-level jobs inside their own companies to discover big problems and understand the everyday struggles of their front-line employees.

As the TV show and Khosrowshahi's experience demonstrate, in a world where it is increasingly possible to insulate ourselves from how things get made or done, it's all too easy to miss out on the insights that come from doing things ourselves. When we immerse ourselves in tasks we typically don't do, we can gain a deeper understanding of the processes, intricacies, and challenges involved. We also build empathy for the people who are doing those tasks.

{ Doing something yourself offers invaluable lessons you may not learn through observation alone. }

For example, several years ago, Rohit was invited to deliver a keynote for a company in the heating, ventilation, and air conditioning (HVAC) industry. In the weeks leading up to his talk, he asked if the team could arrange a visit to a local repair shop where he could watch an HVAC installation and join a technician on a repair job. While, sadly, Rohit didn't walk away from the experience able to fix an HVAC system himself, he did have a better idea about the daily stresses and frustrations HVAC repair professionals experience. And having some experience of the challenges they faced allowed Rohit to deliver a more personal and relevant talk for that audience.

Similarly, Ben believes that the best way for his venture capital fund to understand new investment opportunities is to regularly make customer introductions before they invest. If his firm can find potential customers and listen to the companies who pitched them, they can earn a deeper understanding of the pain they are solving and make each company's approach different. Additionally, dedicating themselves to always making these sorts of introductions grows their community and generates goodwill in the process.

This approach has been so successful they chose to take it a step further by committing to help *every* company they invest in to gain new customers.

You don't need to listen to thousands of pitches or repair an HVAC system yourself, but there is no substitute for getting your hands dirty. Whenever you can, choose to *do something* instead of just reading about it or watching a video.

HOW TO
Get Your Hands Dirty

Get Physical

Volunteer to do hands-on work for a charitable organization, like helping build homes or planting a community garden. Or do a small DIY project in your home, like changing the wiring on a light switch. As you do these tasks, try to focus on the details of  how they are done, the steps involved, and the skills necessary. Any chance to take on a task outside your comfort zone can be an opportunity to discover new insights that you might not find any other way.

Be an Assistant

Arrange a "ride along" with one of your friends or family members to assist them for a day. Shadowing someone in an industry different from yours could offer powerful lessons and insights. Even if there is no "do-

ing" (or car ride!) involved, getting a bird's-eye view of someone else's work as a close observer can offer you a different perspective than what you would ever be able to learn if you were not there in person.

UNCOVER INSIGHTS

Ask Story Questions

Hone Your Nunchi

Get Your Hands Dirty

Spot Natural Wisdom

Find the Right Room

Step Into Others' Shoes

Spot Natural Wisdom

An observation during a golf game would change Mick Pearce's life. As an architect based in Zimbabwe, Pearce was working on a new commission for an office building in Harare when he noticed some termite mounds on the side of the course. They were impossible to miss. Sometimes growing to over 100 feet wide and 30 feet high, termite mounds are the tallest structures on Earth built by non-human creatures. To regulate airflow and maintain an ideal temperature of 86 degrees Fahrenheit all year round, the termites integrate an ingeniously complex series of holes in the outer layers of the mounds.

Intrigued by this natural design, Pearce wondered if a similar concept might help him create a self-ventilating building for people. The Eastgate Centre, which he built drawing inspiration from the termite mounds, features two towers connected by an atrium with a duct system that pushes hot air through the building's chimneys. Its award-winning design cost 10 percent less than conventional buildings and requires no air-conditioning system.

Pearce's innovative architectural solution is a classic example of biomimicry—the practice of adapting an occurrence found in nature to solve a human need. There are plenty of modern stories of this innovation philosophy in action. Engineers in Japan shaped a bullet train engine after the beak of a kingfisher bird to lower fuel consumption. The aerospace firm Lockheed Martin modeled a new drone rotor design on the way maple seeds spin in the air as they fall. And a Swiss engineer famously invented Velcro after discovering burrs sticking to his socks when he returned from a hike.

But you don't need to be a wildly creative architect or an engineer on a life-changing hike to find inspiration and uncover useful insights in nature. You can practice a more everyday form of biomimicry by seeking your own inspiration from the natural world around you.

{ Tapping into nature's wisdom can open the door to discovering new insights from unexpected sources around us. }

Observing nature's patterns—such as the changing seasons or the life cycles of plants—can offer ideas for how we might deal with or manage change ourselves.

Nature can be a profound source of insight and inspiration at every level and often has been in the past. For example, seeing various animals and their methods of camouflage to hide from predators has inspired a wide range of gear for military uses and outdoor enthusiasts also looking to disguise themselves in the wild.

By cultivating a practice of mindful observation of the natural world, we can harness its wisdom and gain unexpected insights to help solve any challenge we are facing. The key is taking time to notice these easy-to-ignore clues that have been there all along.

HOW TO
Spot Natural Wisdom

Consider the Full System

Nature is full of systems that work unexpectedly. If you consider them in isolation, you'd think too much shade or uncontrolled forest fires are both undesirable in nature. Yet it is actually an ex-

cess of sun that can be deadly for certain plants. Some trees require extreme heat from fire for their seeds to germinate. To appreciate these contradictions, you must shift your focus to the larger system. What seems negative or detrimental at first (like too much shade or a forest fire) may prove to be a necessity in the long run.

See the Bark

While the big picture can offer unique context for nature, the opposite is also true. Just as you can miss seeing the forest for the trees, you can miss seeing the detail in nature too. Next time you are outside, make a list of 10 things you had never noticed before. Which plants seem to be thriving and which are not? What detail did you see that was there all along but you only now noticed?

UNCOVER INSIGHTS

Ask Story Questions

Hone Your Nunchi

Get Your Hands Dirty

Spot Natural Wisdom

Find the Right Room

Step Into Others' Shoes

Find the Right Room

For a few days in 1999, a small group of scientists and thinkers huddled inside a room in a nondescript Santa Monica hotel to predict what the future would look like. The exact list of participants was never released.

They had all been invited by legendary filmmaker Steven Spielberg to help him and his production team craft a realistic portrayal of the future for an upcoming project. In the end, many of the ideas brainstormed over that one weekend were brought to life in the 2001 film *Minority Report*, now considered a modern science-fiction classic.

The movie was the first to portray many elements of the future that are now rapidly becoming reality: self-driving cars, computers that operate by hand motions, aggressively personalized ad targeting, smart thermostats, and biometric entry systems, to name a few. The film has been so eerily accurate that many observers have suggested maybe the movie actually inspired the future instead of the other way around.

Of course, most of us don't have the ability to summon the world's smartest people to help us with our projects like Spielberg can. But there is a broader lesson we can take away from this: sometimes the best way to uncover insights is to be part of the right room so you can be inspired by the right people.

This desire to bring innovative ideas and people together fueled the first Non-Obvious Dinner more than two decades ago. Tired of surface conversations at networking events, Ben decided to host the sort of dinner he wished he could attend: one where conversations went beyond the obvious. In 2002 at the Wilmington Club in Delaware, the first edition of this annual tradition gathered nearly one hundred attendees, including CEOs of large companies, up-and-coming entrepreneurs, and even the governor of Delaware. Everyone at the dinner was asked to answer a single question: *What's your non-obvious idea that could change the world?*

The question wasn't just meant as an icebreaker. The shared goal of the evening was to find the *best* non-obvious idea, as voted on by the rest of the participants in the room. One winning idea proposed teaching drone piloting in public schools so students can learn at a young age what is likely to become an in-demand trade vocation for the future. Another suggested that privacy would become the new luxury in an increasingly data-driven world—a prediction that has already come true.

Over the years, these annual dinners have gathered hundreds of the smartest minds in business, politics, academia, and science to discuss non-obvious ideas. To ensure diversity of participants, Ben and his team have included high school students and graduates of a diverse list of universities to participate alongside artists, doctors, educators, and non-profit founders.

The ideas that were born every year from curating these people in a room together were similarly impressive and support the notion that finding face-to-face perspective-shifting conversations, even as our world gets more and more digital, is a powerful way to uncover insights. And there is no substitute for being in a room like that.

HOW TO
Find the Right Room

Attend Think Sessions

Many people host gatherings of people (often called *salons*) to discuss interesting ideas. Getting an invitation to one of these often starts with personal connections, but you can also go  outside the people you know by attending local meetups and looking at local networking groups, business clubs, and industry associations. After exploring these options, if you still don't find any interesting or available events to join—maybe it's a sign you should host your own!

Expand Your Professional Development

The world is filled with opportunities for professional learning and network building. Rather than just focusing on events in your industry or limiting yourself to your current interests, what if you expanded your search?

Engage your curiosity. Join a friend to attend an event about their passion which you know little about. Sometimes finding the right room just requires opening a nearby door instead of walking right past it.

UNCOVER INSIGHTS

Ask Story Questions

Hone Your Nunchi

Get Your Hands Dirty

Spot Natural Wisdom

Find the Right Room

Step Into Others' Shoes

Step Into Others' Shoes

Magazines are one of the most personalized forms of media. They know exactly who they are written for and what their audience cares about. Whether you are a current subscriber to any periodicals or not, chances are you can name at least a handful of magazines you have read at some point.

But it's also likely that you've never picked up one that does not align with your interests. *Teen Vogue. Modern Farmer. Delayed Gratification. Monocle. Lighthouse Digest.* There are nearly 7,500 magazines in circulation in the United States alone. Together with niche publications such as industry catalogs, regional newspapers, or published thought leadership pieces from trade industries, they make up an accessible goldmine of information about people with interests different from your own that are seldom appreciated or consumed by anyone outside their community.

If you pick up a magazine or newspaper or catalog that is new to you, the articles might open your eyes to issues that you had never considered. The photos featured can introduce you to celebrities you have never heard of. The ads might present products you did not know existed or would never buy. Perusing these publications can reveal deep insights into what drives and inspires groups of people whose beliefs differ from yours.

{ Magazines and immersive experiences offer a uniquely captivating glimpse into the passions of people different from you. }

Beyond print media, digital media can also can offer similar and even more immersive ways to extend your understanding of others. Virtual reality, in particular, has been lauded as an "empathy engine" thanks to its visceral ability to help users shift their perspective and take on someone else's. Today, users can don a headset to immerse themselves in a virtual experience that simulates being a refugee in a holding camp or a prisoner incarcerated in solitary confinement. Inside gaming studios, full-body haptic suits even allow wearers to experience simulations of physical experiences like being punched or the weight of a backpack on your shoulders.

Life doesn't offer most of us enough moments to understand people who think, believe, and live differently than we do. Buying a magazine focused on an unfamiliar topic is something any of us can do for less than ten dollars. While immersive virtual experiences are not as ubiquitous as magazines, they are also becoming more accessible and affordable every day.

Media and experiences like these can help us understand the lives and circumstances of others in an intensely human and unforgettable way. They pave the way for feeling genuine empathy for their lived experience in a way that reading an article *about* them or watching a documentary may not. Being able to step into unfamiliar shoes allows us to think beyond our assumptions, biases, and limitations, opening us up to see what we might miss otherwise.

HOW TO
Step Into Others' Shoes

Follow Your Un-Interests

Find a magazine, book, documentary, or TV series on a topic you have no interest in. Maybe even one that you dislike. Not interested in clothes or fash-  ion? Stream a documentary about an iconic designer. A loyal member of a political party? Read a book or blog written by someone whose political beliefs you disagree with. Choosing to engage your curiosity around your "un-interests" can lead to some of the most unexpected insights, and open your mind in a way that can invite more non-obvious insights to emerge.

Make More Weak Ties

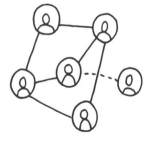

Social media is really good at surfacing perspectives we agree with from people who think like us. Any new connection is immediately validated to us in terms of how many shared connections we already have. What if you accepted more weak ties—connections with people who know very few (or none) of your current connections already? These people can truly expand your network and thinking the most because they are outside your current circle of friends or colleagues.

PART THREE

Focus Your Ideas

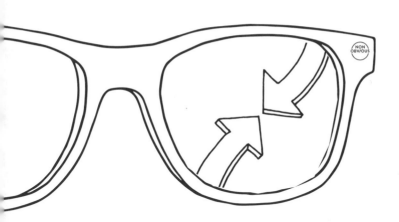

FOCUS YOUR IDEAS

Every May in the southern fields of Turkey's Anatolian province, dozens of family farmers start their mornings picking the softest blooming rose petals that will later be steam distilled into their  world-renowned Damascus rose oil. It takes more than 10,000 flowers to make a single drop of this precious oil, worth more per ounce than gold. This combination of time—and a lot of raw material—creates a world-class product.

The 250-year-old Waterford crystal factory in Ireland is renowned for its long-standing program where those who  aspire to become master craftsmen must complete an eight-year-long apprenticeship to learn how to make every cut in glass required to create the brand's high-end luxury crystal bowls, vases, and glasses. When they are done with their training, these master craftsmen, like the Turkish family farmers, use a unique method of distillation to take many elements and focus them to create a beautiful, elaborate, and very specific product.

Focus, the third step of the SIFT method, also involves a similar process of distillation. Our favorite analogy to describe this is through a term that is usually associated with museums: curation.

{ **The art of curation is about discerning what is most meaningful.** }

Museum curators don't just create exhibits, they also routinely decide what not to showcase. What paintings should be moved to the archives? What treasures should be packed away because they don't fit the theme of an exhibit?

Like museum curators, most of us will face similar challenges in refining our own thinking. After following the techniques from the first two steps of the SIFT method, you'll already have created space for new ideas  and uncovered some insights. Deciding which of these to focus on can become overwhelming—but it doesn't need to be. One thing that can help is to become what science fiction author Isaac Asimov famously described as a "speed understander," someone adept at quickly separating the signal from the noise.

In this section, we'll show you how to focus your ideas on what's most important so you can become a speed understander for yourself.

FOCUS YOUR IDEAS

Identify the Real Problem

Discover the Water

Be a Satisficer

See the Other Side

Add Constraints

Use Augmented Creativity

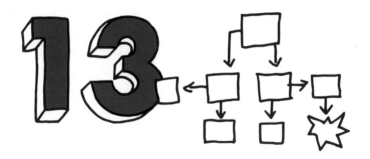

Identify the Real Problem

Elisha Otis didn't invent the elevator, but his name is the one most associated with the humble mode of indoor transportation used by people around the world every day.

What he *did* create—and demonstrate dramatically at the 1853 World's Fair in New York was the first passenger-safe elevator. Before his invention, elevators were widely used, but never to transport people. The danger of a cable snapping and sending passengers hurtling to a fiery death meant people were scared to ride in an elevator.

At the World's Fair that year, Otis climbed onto an open platform elevator as a man stood behind him, ominously holding an axe. At just the right scripted moment, the staged saboteur cut the rope as onlookers gasped in horror. Rather than plunging to his death, Otis and the platform came to an abrupt halt thanks to the safety brakes he had installed. It was, historically and literally, the world's first elevator pitch.

{ **Often, the path to non-obvious thinking starts with focusing on solving the right problem.** }

After Otis's theatrical demonstration, the safety brake was quickly adopted widely, and the elevator became, in the words of author and economist Tim Harford, one of the "fifty inventions that shaped the modern economy." It brought about a new era in architecture, allowing buildings to be taller and, in turn, cities to be more densely populated.

The mantra of modern entrepreneurship follows in Otis's footsteps: fall in love with problems rather than solutions. But the problem that truly needs addressing is often more nuanced than it appears. In the case of the elevator, at face value, the problem Otis was solving was fixing the danger inherent in riding on an elevator. His innovation, the safety brake, did just that.

The *real* problem, though, was convincing a wary market that his innovation was dependable enough for elevator riders to trust it with their lives. *That* was the problem he solved with his memorable World's Fair stunt.

A related problem-solving mindset can also be seen in the healthcare field. Many pain management doctors, for example, are now making it a priority to focus on underlying medical issues instead of rushing to prescribe pharmaceutical solutions to alleviate pain. These evolved doctors already know that pain is the human body's way of sending a message, and they are committing themselves to listening. The choice to either ignore or address these signals can mean the difference between potentially leading a patient toward a painkiller addiction or offering them a better way to manage chronic pain.

In most challenging situations there are likely to be surface problems and hidden ones. Building your skills to dig deeper to spot and spend your attention on those masked issues is a skill often associated with consultants. What they do is ask smart questions and learn from the answers to identify the real problem where they should spend their focus. Let's review a few techniques to help you do that.

HOW TO
Identify the Real Problem

Follow Your Frustrations

Let your frustration be a source of inspiration. Getting to the root cause of what annoys you can help point your focus in the right direction. Many of the founding stories for brands we recognize today started in this way. Reed Hastings famously had the idea for Netflix after getting frustrated by a $40 fee from Blockbuster for returning a video late.

When you choose to take inspiration from the things that make you angry for being the way they are, it can help you to achieve a focus that leads to better non-obvious thinking.

Ask Five Whys

Next time you need to uncover an underlying problem to focus your ideas, use the "five whys method"—asking why something is the way  it is and following each explanation with the same question: asking "Why?" five times. Popularized by Toyota founder Sakichi Toyoda, this thinking model can also help you get to the *real* underlying problem faster and discover your focus in the process.

FOCUS YOUR IDEAS

Identify the Real Problem

Discover the Water

Be a Satisficer

See the Other Side

Add Constraints

Use Augmented Creativity

Discover the Water

The search for alien life is a relatively recent one in the long timeline of human existence. Thousands of years ago, our ancestors likely wondered about the stars in the sky but knew little, if anything, about solar systems. Today, our growing understanding of space has led many in the scientific community and beyond to believe in the possibility of life beyond our planet.

A cornerstone of the search for alien life is the "Goldilocks zone," a term first coined more than fifty years ago to describe the theory that every star in the galaxy must have a region where conditions are neither too hot nor too cold—but *just right*—to sustain liquid water, which is still believed to be a prerequisite for all organic life (as we know it) to exist.

In other words, rather than broadly searching for signals of alien life, it is more efficient to focus on the search for planets in a habitable zone where liquid water might be present. Find the water, and we might find the aliens too.

Just as astronomers identified water as the key indicator of possible alien life, looking for the common theme or pattern among your insights and ideas can help you focus on those that matter most.

> { Pinpointing a common element among ideas can help you zero in on the bigger picture. }

That's an approach Rohit took when writing the final *Megatrends* edition of his signature Non-Obvious Trend book series as well. For that project, he had to identify the most prominent themes across the 125+ trends he had previously introduced over the past ten years. To start, he focused on a trend from the 2011 report, where he had suggested that social media was making celebrities more accessible. In the following years, other trends noted how companies had started showcasing their employees as heroes, how luxury brands were trying to be more relatable, why products with flaws were beloved *because* of their quirks, and how creating more human experiences was becoming a driver of innovation at companies of all sizes.

The common theme among these trends was something he described as *human mode*—a term describing the idea that as our world gets increasingly digital, people are seeking out and placing greater value on physical, authentic, and sometimes imperfect experiences designed with empathy and delivered by humans.

Rohit's trend curation method and the quest to find water on distant worlds are both examples of how identifying a common element can help you align multiple ideas, especially those that may not immediately seem to have anything that binds them.

Seek that common element among your insights to focus on what really matters. That is how you find *your* water.

HOW TO
Discover the Water

Focus on Similarities

When engaging with people from cultures other than your own, finding shared experiences, values, and interests leads to common ground. Empathy starts with trying to identify bigger similarities instead of getting distracted and disconnected by differences. Music is often described as the universal language, and nearly every culture on Earth has some sort of drums or percussion to create the beat. It is a perfect analogy. You don't need musical abilities to hear the beat. You just need to listen for it.

Go Physical

To better identify what your ideas have in common, sometimes physically laying them out can help. Use a  whiteboard, a digital collaborative platform, or just a table and a stack of stories and ads torn from magazines and spread out where you can visually arrange them. The stories and ideas that we can touch and hold as part of this process become more meaningful for us simply because they feel rarer than digital content.

FOCUS YOUR IDEAS

Identify the Real Problem

Discover the Water

Be a Satisficer

See the Other Side

Add Constraints

Use Augmented Creativity

Be a Satisficer

One of the most influential books in the social science and marketing fields just turned twenty years old. When it was first published, it challenged the fundamental belief about consumption that having more choices is always good.

Barry Schwartz's *The Paradox of Choice* stunned the business world by suggesting that too many choices can *diminish* happiness and increase anxiety. In the book, Schwartz showed that the more time we spend deciding on a purchase, the more regret we are likely to feel about it. In a sense, the book predicted FOMO (fear of missing out) entering the dictionary.

One of the main ideas from the book is that most people are *maximizers* or *satisficers*, depending on the situation. Maximizers "seek and accept only the best," often feeling the need to spend hours researching and weighing their options to ensure a decision or purchase is the optimal one. Paradoxically, maximizers also score high on the regret scale—a tool psychologists use to measure how much remorse someone feels over a past decision.

Even when maximizers end up with a decision or outcome that is objectively better, they often struggle to be happy with their choices and feel the need to know how the alternative choices might have turned out.

> Learning to appreciate when an idea is good enough instead of always seeking more options can be the key to focus.

In contrast, satisficers "settle for something that is good enough and do not worry about the possibility that there might be something better." You might think being a satisficer means being willing to settle for something suboptimal, but Schwartz points out that satisficers are just as discriminating as maximizers. Being a satisficer, according to Schwartz, is the secret to "fighting back against the tyranny of overwhelming choices."

From sitting down on the couch and trying to decide what show to stream to encountering twenty-eight (or more!) brands of pasta sauce in the grocery store, the chaos of too many options has invaded nearly every part of our lives. Deciding where to focus will be considerably easier if you can learn to think like a satisficer. Adopting this mindset isn't really about making better choices;  it's about committing to the choices you've *already* made. Satisficers don't dwell on the other options they *could* have made. Instead, they double down on the ones they *did* make. They can make them work.

Besides helping you avoid decision paralysis, a satisficer mindset allows you to focus on an idea without regrets and devote yourself to fully understanding and developing it—and perhaps seeing something in the process that others have missed.

HOW TO
Be a Satisficer

Be a Chooser, Not a Picker

What criteria do you use to make a choice? It probably depends on the choice, but science suggests the important thing is to make sure you have some criteria 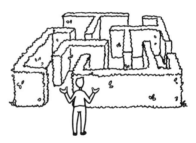 in mind. Schwartz explains that actively considering your options will make you a "chooser" instead of a "picker." A picker feels overloaded by choice. A chooser focuses on what makes a decision important and imagines alternatives if necessary, but then moves forward without regret or imagining every other foregone choice they could have made. Be a chooser.

Decide Who to Trust

When you are faced with a decision with many options, sometimes the only way to simplify your choice is to seek advice from the person you feel you can trust the most on the topic. Find the right expertise—or spend your time deciding whose advice you trust the most. Then seek out their perspective and consider their recommendations. This can be the ideal way to narrow your focus in situations where there are many variables and you might struggle to make a choice without some guidance.

FOCUS YOUR IDEAS

Identify the Real Problem

Discover the Water

Be a Satisficer

See the Other Side

Add Constraints

Use Augmented Creativity

FOCUS YOUR IDEAS //

See the Other Side

Quick! What do you see? A duck or a rabbit?

This century-old optical illusion has long been a tool for re-searchers trying to understand the human brain. Some teams theorized that the animal you see first could indicate which side of your brain is more dominant. Others suggested that the speed with which you *alternate* between seeing the duck and the rabbit might reveal your brain flexibility.

One research team went in a different direction, testing a hypothesis that the animal you see first might be influenced by the seasons. Their results suggested that around Easter time, more people were likely to see the rabbit. At other times of year, the duck was reportedly more popular.

$$\left\{ \begin{array}{l} \text{There is more than one way to see} \\ \text{something; seeing it from a different} \\ \text{perspective is the real challenge.} \end{array} \right\}$$

Over a century of multiple studies, one thing has never been in dispute—*both answers are right.* In our divided modern times, it's hard to imagine this conclusion being accepted by anyone. People cannot decide what the truth actually means, but they do seem certain that they are right and others are wrong. What if the ability to hold two contradicting ideas in equal regard was actually the real truth?

While the science remains inconclusive about what optical illusions like this one actually reveal about us or our brains, they do remind us that there is usually another way to see something—a way you didn't see at first.

In the 1990s, the Magic Eye book series featured stereograms—flat images where a hidden 3D image was integrated into a two-dimensional pattern. The only way to see these buried images was by altering your focus so you looked *through* the page instead of directly at it. While the popularity of these Magic Eye images has faded, they still offer an enduring lesson for how we might see the other harder-to-notice side of anything if we just focus on a different angle.

The most important thing is not which side of the optical illusion you see first or even how quickly you can find the hidden message in the Magic Eye, but if you even see it. And whether you can appreciate the perspective of those who seem certain everyone is just pretending to see something and there is actually nothing there at all.

HOW TO
See the Other Side

Embrace Dual Truths

In a world where we are constantly tempted to see things as either true or false, there is a lightness that comes from being able to accept the gray area. That image is a duck *and*  a rabbit. A platypus is an animal that is both a mammal and a reptile. A glass can be both half full and half empty. Embracing the possibility that two or more things that seem incompatible can be true simultaneously is a sophisticated idea. But if you start paying close attention, you'll find that this is the case in many more instances than you'd think possible.

Tell Situational Backstories

When encountering a rude person who makes you angry, ask yourself: *What situation could make this behavior reasonable?* For example, if someone cuts you off in traffic, imagine they are rushing to the hospital for an emergency. Psychologists suggest this technique helps you consider the other side of any situation and choose to live your life offering more understanding and kindness even to the people who wrong you.

FOCUS YOUR IDEAS

Identify the Real Problem

Discover the Water

Be a Satisficer

See the Other Side

Add Constraints

Use Augmented Creativity

FOCUS YOUR IDEAS //

Add Constraints

One of the most well-known doctors in modern history owes his fame to a chance stroll on Madison Avenue.

Ted, as he was known to his friends, had given himself the title of "doctor" despite having no medical training. He dreamed of being a published author, but was discouraged by a string of twenty-seven rejections from book publishers.

Finally, in 1937, as he was walking down the street, he bumped into a former classmate who happened to work for a publisher named Vanguard Press. This friend agreed to give Ted a shot and publish his first book, *And to Think That I Saw It on Mulberry Street*. The story was an instant hit, propelling Dr. Seuss to household-name status.

Over a decade later, Dr. Seuss's then-editor, William Spaulding, had an idea. In the 1950s, inspiring kids to enjoy reading was getting harder and harder. Television was presenting an irresistible alternative, and children were abandoning books. Spaulding challenged Ted to write a story "that first-graders can't put down"—using no more than 225 different words from a pre-determined list of 348. Rising to the task, Dr. Seuss wrote *The Cat in the Hat* using 236 words.

A few years later, another friend took that same challenge one step further, daring Dr. Seuss to write a children's book using only *50* unique words. His answer to *that* test would become the bestselling book of his prolific career, *Green Eggs and Ham.*

> { Constraints can force you to be more creative by pushing you to do more with less. }

Like *The Cat in the Hat* and *Green Eggs and Ham*, some of history's most enduring creative works were created by introducing similarly beneficial constraints. Near the end of his life, renowned artist Henri Matisse was confined to his bed and wheelchair. Unable to stand and paint any longer, he created a new artistic diversion: paper cutouts. Many years later, some of his best-known art was produced through this method he later described as "drawing with scissors."

In the mid-1980s, legendary Nintendo game music composer Koji Kondo developed the soundtrack for the original Super Mario Brothers game while facing extreme constraints of his own. Under orders to use as little data storage as possible, he composed the music using just five repeating tones that were looped in unexpected ways in order to avoid boring or annoying gamers. Today, it is widely considered one of the best video game soundtracks of all time.

Constraints like the ones each of these creators faced can force better ideas *because* they offer some structure around creativity. Science has shown that people tend to develop more varied and creative solutions when options are limited.

As you turn your attention to curating your ideas, consider imposing a few creative constraints of your own. For example, what if you could restrict your ideas to only what might be possible within a specific industry or what could reasonably be accomplished within no more than 48 hours? Remember, when you are forced to innovate with less, you can focus your thinking in new and interesting ways.

HOW TO
Add Constraints

Practice the Art of Subtraction

As the writer Antoine de Saint-Exupéry famously said, "A designer knows he has achieved perfection not when there is nothing left to add, but when there is nothing left to take away." Embrace this philosophy by limiting your idea development time or reducing the number of people involved in a decision. You can also introduce constraints around the technology you will (or won't) use, or the budget you make available. Each of these choices are examples of sharpening your focus through intentional subtraction.

Invite Brevity

Twitter's original 140-character limit required early users to distill their thoughts. It sparked a new method of communication. The mandatory limit did not allow for much nuance, but it helped users to focus only on  what mattered most. You can adopt a similar approach by being as brief as possible and choosing to use more plain language in all your communications—from emails to contracts.

Identify the Real Problem

Discover the Water

Be a Satisficer

See the Other Side

Add Constraints

Use Augmented Creativity

Use Augmented Creativity

Charley Douglass had a secret the size of a mini refrigerator on wheels.

Across nearly every large Hollywood TV studio in the 1950s and '60s, Douglass was considered the maestro of laughter. His signature "Laff Box," a contraption that looked like a typewriter and tiny portable piano with metal strings, could produce hundreds of types of crowd laughter, from surprised chuckles to loud guffaws to a slowly diminishing laughter with one person enjoying the joke just a little longer than everyone else. Driven by its success and the cutthroat competitive nature of the movie business, Douglass was notoriously secretive about how it worked. His secrecy helped him build a monopoly over the laugh track business that lasted for decades. His laughter reels are still in use today.

The Laff Box was designed to mimic the effect of a real-life audience for broadcast television, a new category of entertainment that allowed people to watch a show isolated at home. Douglass helped "sweeten" the television shows by adding a masterful combination of background laughter that TV critics of the time said "gave people permission to laugh." He made funny shows even funnier by helping the audience focus on the jokes.

A laugh track is an example of augmented creativity—a method used to focus on and enhance the creativity of an individual or product. The term sweetening is an apt one to describe how augmented creativity works: it's like adding sugar to a cup of tea.

Today, there are many ways to automate creative augmentation using generative artificial intelligence tools (Gen AI). You can run an AI filter to improve the sound quality of any recording or use it to fill in missing details of a damaged or tightly cropped photo. Or you can generate text or refine your own writing with AI tools, "sweetening" your prose and making it clearer, shorter, or more creative.

As Gen AI continues to become a larger part of our daily lives, workplaces, and any new professional tasks, the challenge to integrate and benefit from it in productive and ethical ways will become more urgent. Yet if you learn to do it well, you will find yourself able to harness a superpower that makes *you* more productive, creative, and prolific.

> Seeking collaboration partners (human or technical) to enhance your creative output can help you focus.

Like the Laff Box, these tools enhance the creativity of your idea. They don't work best as a replacement for creative effort, but rather as collaboration partners.

In that sense, you might leverage AI technology or get help from a colleague to augment your creativity. Either way, what matters is that you can focus your thinking by seeking out creative collaboration partners in human and technology forms.

HOW TO
Use Augmented Creativity

Generate Some Criticism

As we wrote the various chapters for this book, we regularly fed chapters into a Gen AI tool and prompted it to provide a 1-star negative review along

with a criticism of our text. We also asked our Gen AI tool to read and summarize various chapters of the book from several perspectives: including a 19-year-old college student, a startup founder, and a chief marketing officer. This tactic helped us improve the stories. When you are trying to elevate an idea's non-obviousness, you can use these tools in the same way for quick on-demand feedback.

Collaborate More

This book benefited from many voices who added early input, offered feedback on its ideas, and helped to hone these lessons and insights. This collaboration came from events, conversations, interviews, and the many sources that we turned to in writing the book as well as a panel of early readers. When you're feeling a lack of focus or uncertainty about what matters most, seeking out an external perspective can be the key to helping you refine your focus too.

PART FOUR

Define
the Twist

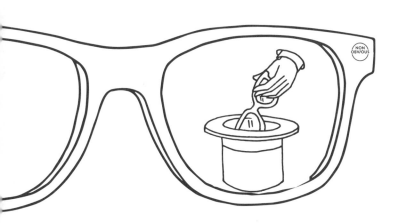

DEFINE THE TWIST

The only difference between a hurricane and a typhoon is where in the world it's happening. They are both forms of a tropical cyclone: a circular storm over water with high winds that form due to low atmospheric pressure.

Nearly 150 years ago, American inventor John M. Finch drew inspiration from these cyclones to build a machine that collected dust inside big spaces. The "cyclonic separator" would go on to be used inside sawmills and other industrial factories for decades.

Many years later, another inventor saw a cyclonic separator at work in one of those sawmills and wondered whether it could be 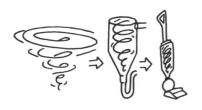 miniaturized. A mini cyclonic separator could be more commercially successful, he thought, and useful to solve everyday problems. After years of experimentation and more than five thousand failed prototypes, he eventually invented the DA001, an upright vacuum cleaner that used a patented "dual cyclone" technology. The D stood for his last name: Dyson.

The fascinating part of this story isn't that James Dyson invented a technology that would power a billion-dollar company and lead to many innovative reinvented versions of household products like hair dryers, heaters, and fans. What's fascinating is that he *didn't*. The cyclonic separator was invented by someone else. Dyson saw its potential in a different way and miniaturized it. In other words, he found the *twist*.

{ Defining the twist is about taking your thoughtful ideas in an unexpected direction. }

The final stage of our SIFT method, defining the twist, is about using your insights to create or imagine something new and original that no one else can or has before.

The twist is where the magic happens, where non-obvious thinking becomes concrete and actionable. In this section, you will learn some of our favorite methods for propelling your thinking in unique new directions, and even turn them into reality.

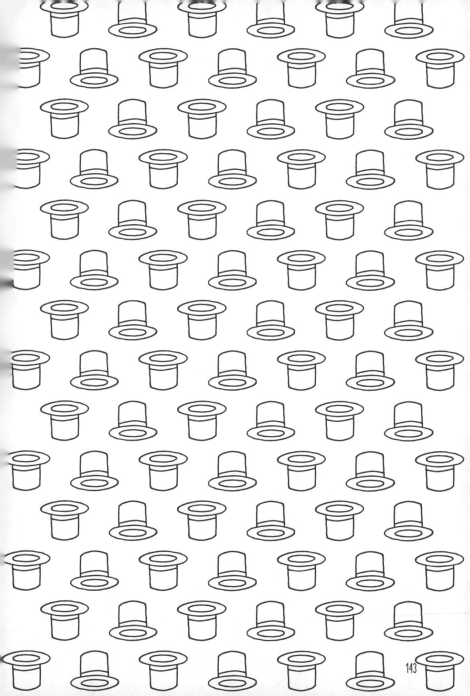

DEFINE THE TWIST

Seek Flip Solutions

Find Option C

Practice Enigmatology

Think Un-Whatever

Mind the Intersections

Create Your Argot

Seek Flip Solutions

Aaron Sams and Jonathan Bergmann were chemistry teachers at a small high school in Colorado when they made an unusual announcement: they would no longer be giving lectures in class.

Instead, they would record their lectures using smartphones and pre-broadcast them for students to watch at home on YouTube. Students without internet access could get the lessons on a flash drive. No computer? No problem. Sams and Bergmann would burn the lessons onto a DVD. No one was left behind.

Back in 2007, the teaching duo were early adopters of a model that reinvented classroom time. Instead of sitting in a room for 50 minutes listening to instruction, students would watch the lectures at home. Then class time would be used for answering questions, having discussions, doing labs, and learning from one-on-one instruction.

These two teachers weren't the first to come up with what has come to be known as the "flipped classroom"—but they were part of the movement to popularize it. Perhaps the biggest accelerating force for this model was the popularity of learning videos posted by the Khan Academy. Founded by education entrepreneur Salman Khan, the free online learning platform now hosts thousands of videos on all sorts of topics to help students of any age learn outside the traditional classroom environment.

This sort of reverse thinking—solving a problem by flipping the rules upside down—can be helpful in many other contexts outside of education. It is also an effective way to define what we mean by a twist. It starts with a deep understanding of the rules behind a system and how things work within it, followed by asking, *what if* we do the exact opposite?

When Vivek Ravisankar first pitched his new business idea to Ben's VC firm, he described resumes as black holes. Given that they consist of a few short bullet points describing previous work experience, they don't help those who are reading them judge someone's actual ability. In a world where many employers cared more about skills than academic pedigree, this seemed backward. What if instead of writing down a list of skills, a person could demonstrate those skills in real-life scenarios?

> Flip the rules upside down to intentionally challenge conventional wisdom and do the opposite of what others do.

The question inspired him to co-found HackerRank, an online platform where developers compete in skills-based challenges posted by companies and employers. The platform allows developers to showcase their skills when applying for jobs, and it has been wildly successful. Forty percent of the world's 60 million software developers are now on the platform, and the company is currently valued at nearly half a billion dollars.

The idea of a merit- and skills-based tool that could replace the traditional resume when hiring software developers is an example of flip thinking.

Like those Colorado schoolteachers or the founders of HackerRank, you can also find a twist by applying flip thinking, but you must be willing to question how things are currently being done—and have the courage to turn the status quo on its head.

HOW TO
Seek Flip Solutions

Try It Backward

Doing something in the opposite way to how it is "always" done can give you an unusual perspective. For example, many hiking trails in parks offer a circuit with a suggested direc-

tion. What if you followed those arrows backward? Taking a trail in reverse could offer a unique perspective on an otherwise well-worn path. You could use a similar philosophy to approach any professional or personal challenge too. Can you solve a problem with *less* collaboration? What if you could sell more products by *raising* your prices? Asking yourself these sorts of inverted questions can help you spot new ways to solve problems.

Do the Unthinkable

Quirky ecommerce shoe seller Zappos. com used to pay people $4,000 to quit, based on their belief (and plenty of industry data) that it was cheaper to incentivize new workers to leave earlier than to have them stay in a role they are unhappy doing. It worked so well, the company became a human resources case study and their fiercely loyal workforce and legendarily kind customer service was a key reason why Amazon spent $1.2 billion to acquire the brand in 2009. Paying people to leave flips the model for onboarding because it is unthinkable. Learning to flip your thinking can also start with the same question: What would your *unthinkable* change look like?

DEFINE THE TWIST

Seek Flip Solutions

Find Option C

Practice Enigmatology

Think Un-Whatever

Mind the Intersections

Create Your Argot

Find Option C

Despite being unknown by most in the West, Genrikh Altshuller spent his life formulating a method that has helped thousands of people solve problems more creatively.

His journey began with an obsession over patent applications. After poring through hundreds of thousands of them, he shaped a firm belief that the key to a more prosperous society was encouraging and teaching everyone how to be creative. Unfortunately, his ideas were at odds with the communist Soviet regime he was living under at the time.

Naively believing his insights could sway policy, he sent an ill-fated letter to Joseph Stalin suggesting Soviet schools and factories teach creative problem-solving. Stalin wasn't as open-minded as Altshuller had hoped. He was arrested, charged with political crimes, and sentenced to 25 years of hard labor in a Soviet gulag prison near the rim of the Arctic Circle.

After Stalin's death, Altshuller was released and went on to start the groundbreaking Azerbaijan Public Institute of Inventive Creativity. Together with colleagues, he developed a creative thinking method known as TRIZ (a Russian acronym for *Theory of Inventive Problem-Solving*, pronounced "trees"). One of the core principles of this theory was a mental blind spot that Altshuller called "the contradiction."

{ Avoiding limited two-option thinking can help you arrive at nuanced, original third options that others are unable to imagine. }

Altshuller believed that learning to think like an outsider was the key to seeing more than two options and finding a desirable "option C."

William Brouwer, a woodworker, designer, and architect from Boston, is a perfect example of someone who did this. For many years, Brouwer lived in Japan, where he adopted the practice of keeping a rolled mattress in a closet during the day to save space and unfurling it at night to sleep on.

He knew people in America would also love to save space but would never embrace the idea of ditching a bed frame to sleep on a mattress laid out on the floor. So, he invented the S-frame bed, a piece of convertible furniture that could be flattened into a bed or folded into a couch. Today, we know his design as the futon.

The futon is a classic example of an option-C idea. This elegant, blended solution offers the flexibility for an extra bed when needed while eliminating the less hospitable experience of forcing a guest to camp out on a mattress rolled across the floor.

When you go through your day refusing to limit your thinking to the simple options that are easiest to see, you can challenge your mind to start thinking bigger. The only people who see a third option are the ones who choose to ask why it doesn't exist in the first place.

HOW TO
Find Option C

See Beyond Binary Choices

When presented with choices that seem black or white, imagine a third option. When Rohit first launched the Non-Obvious Book Awards, he used this technique to create a twist by rejecting the traditional topic ar-

☐ ORANGE
☐ APPLE
‒ ‒ ‒ ‒ ‒ ‒ ‒ ‒
☐ *other*

eas such as sales and leadership. Instead, the awards honor a more interesting and diverse list of winners by using unusual categories like most important, most useful, most entertaining, most shareable, and most original.

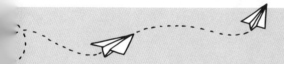

Think Hybrid

Finding the best mix of two options can lead you to a hybrid
solution. One example is a sec-
tor of the book industry known
as hybrid publishing. This is a

relatively new model where authors forego an initial advance
and take on more financial responsibility for publishing their
books in exchange for a much higher percentage of royalties
and more control over the final book. For many authors, including us, this hybrid solution is the ideal option C that incor-
porates the best elements of traditional publishing alongside
the greater flexibility and control over the final end product.

DEFINE THE TWIST

Seek Flip Solutions

Find Option C

Practice Enigmatology

Think Un-Whatever

Mind the Intersections

Create Your Argot

Practice Enigmatology

The world's first college degree in enigmatology—the study of puzzles—was awarded in 1974 to an aspiring puzzle maker from Indiana named Will Shortz. Nearly fifty years later, his work has reached millions of people and is beloved across the world.

Shortz is the crossword puzzle editor for the *New York Times*, a role that requires him to come up with more than 16,000 clues every year. In interviews about his puzzle making technique, he talks about the importance of making clues "twisty," that is, a clue might point to a certain direction while the answer ends up going in a very different one. Using his exhaustive library of puzzles—the world's largest private one—as inspiration, Shortz is always thinking about how to transform the common into the mysterious.

Great puzzle clues and answers often take something we already know and shift how it is presented or what it means. For example, in the final rounds of the 2012 American Crossword Puzzle Tournament, one of the puzzles was titled "Boustrophedon." Named after an ancient form of writing in which one reads each line in alternating directions, the puzzle required competitors to answer questions about "things that move from left to right and back" (like mowing the lawn or dot matrix printers).

> Developing your ideas with a puzzle maker's mindset allows you to make the known unknown (and irresistible) again.

The "Boustrophedon" puzzle was a hit precisely because it forced solvers to think in a new way about something they were already familiar with. It's also a great example of a puzzle maker taking the known and making it new to offer an irresistible challenge.

The invention of the skateboard is most often attributed to Larry Stevenson, the California-based publisher of a surfing magazine, who imagined a "scooter without handles" to appeal to surfers ready to move their sport onto land.

In 1963, Stevenson introduced the first skateboard design with a kicktail—an upward curve on the back of the skateboard that added much-needed control to allow skaters to do the sorts of tricks, jumps, and pivots that led to the popularity of the board. The skateboard drew inspiration from something known—the surfboard—but Stevenson's twist made it different and irresistible.

The same principles that legendary puzzle makers use to reinvent what people know into something more delightful, helped Larry Stevenson pioneer a new form of transportation and diversion that would go on to become a cultural icon and even earn a coveted slot as an exhibition sport in the Summer Olympic games.

Using enigmatology means drawing inspiration from what is already there and then applying a twist to make it unique and lasting.

HOW TO Practice Enigmatology

Assign Meaning to Trivia

The Belgian beer makers behind Stella Artois took the humble beer glass and transformed it into the iconic "chalice" with a gold-plated rim—making it central to the beer-drinking experience the brand promotes. Any beer maker *could*

have done this, but it is now recognizable as part of the Stella experience. Marketers use this technique often, to sell everything from shampoo to breakfast cereal. You can use it too, as a way to create your own twist.

Go Beyond the Easy Answer

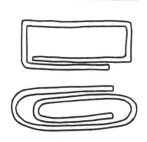

Just as a puzzle maker would not offer easy clues, you can choose to go beyond the easy solutions. Near the end of the 19th century, most people were satisfied to bundle papers with ribbon or string. Norwegian inventor Johan Vaaler could have done the same but instead he was the first to patent a sophisticated yet elegant design for the paper clip. Thinking like an inventor can help you to seek out similar opportunities to find clever, reinvented ways of doing things. A twist might be simple, but like the eventual solution to a good puzzle, it shouldn't be "easy."

DEFINE THE TWIST

Seek Flip Solutions

Find Option C

Practice Enigmatology

Think Un-Whatever

Mind the Intersections

Create Your Argot

DEFINE THE TWIST //

Think Un-Whatever

Back in 2002, Taco Bell was one of the only major fast-food restaurants not serving burgers. Leaning into this difference, their marketing cleverly asked customers to "think outside the bun," a tagline that worked because it offered a perfect reminder of exactly what Taco Bell was *not*: another burger chain.

When automaker Hummer—which got its start making heavy, military-grade vehicles—entered the civilian market, it celebrated the car's oversized and unabashedly self-centered personality with a splashy campaign fronted by action star Arnold Schwarzenegger. It launched with the controversial declaration that the vehicle could help men "reclaim [their] masculinity." The campaign made clear that Hummer's product wasn't reasonable or polite like other cars on the road. It was in-your-face and chauvinistic on purpose.

> Defining your thinking and ideas as the opposite of the status quo can successfully offer a twist that sets them apart.

Years ago, the Hans Brinker Budget Hostel in Amsterdam had an unusual marketing strategy: They promoted themselves as the undisputed "worst hotel in the world." Their posters proudly declared their prowess at everything from losing bags to providing substandard bedding. They boasted that their "games room" was a Post-it Note with a tic-tac-toe grid drawn on it. Despite these promises of a disastrous experience, the property was nearly always sold out.

While other hostels advertised their amenities, Hans Brinker made sure travelers knew the story they would take home after staying there would be far more memorable than decent sheets. What intrepid traveler backpacking across Europe *wouldn't* want to stay at the world's worst hostel and share that story with friends?

Taco Bell, Hummer, and Hans Brinker all took an approach to standing out that you might call an "un-whatever" strategy. This method works because it involves positioning your ideas against something else. Unlike flip thinking, which promotes reversing your mindset, the idea of thinking un-whatever is about defining something based on its opposite. No one was selling fast food that wasn't burgers. No one was making big gas-guzzling cars that celebrated a disdain for environmental or cost issues—the same issues that most other car manufacturers assumed would matter most to car buyers. No one was advertising their property as the worst (but most infamous) lodging option in Amsterdam.

Ask yourself, "What is the argument that no one else in my field, industry, or community would *ever* make?" The answer might lead you in a fascinating, non-obvious direction and help you define a twist that others will almost certainly miss.

HOW TO
Think Un-Whatever

Rethink What Will "Never" Change

Business experts advise focusing on what will never change when defining a longer-term strategy. To define the twist, you can challenge those assumptions of what will never change in your industry or market. For example, Harley-Davidson focused on men for decades until they realized many women love motorcycles, too. They pivoted their marketing to welcome women instead of ignoring them, and today it is the top-selling bike brand among women.

Argue Against a Clear Enemy

Imagine a clear adversary—maybe someone you know in the real world or a fictitious person, idea, or organization. Then commit yourself to be against everything they stand for, believe, and do. This technique can lead you to define a memorable twist. The rapid sales growth of non-dairy milk is a classic example. As a cornerstone of their marketing focus, most makers of oat, nut, and soy milk focus on all the ways milk from cows is a less healthy choice than plant-based alternatives. They have made milk the enemy—and so far it is working.

DEFINE THE TWIST

Seek Flip Solutions

Find Option C

Practice Enigmatology

Think Un-Whatever

Mind the Intersections

Create Your Argot

Mind the Intersections

Project 523 was a secret military task force commissioned by Chinese Chairman Mao Zedong for an unexpected purpose. Named for the date it was founded, May 23, 1967, the project funded more than fifty secret labs across China all working to find a new treatment or vaccine for chloroquine-resistant malaria. For the first two years, the results were underwhelming.

In 1969, there was a turning point in the effort. A scientist named Tu Youyou was put in charge of the program and spent her first two years on the job traveling across China speaking with traditional medicine gurus, visiting remote rainforests, and collecting ancient medical texts.

Thanks to her combined training in modern medicine and traditional Chinese techniques, she also knew that malaria was a disease believed to be older than the human race—so perhaps there was some ancient wisdom that could help. Her instincts paid off. A forgotten treatment detailed in a 1,600-year-old book suggested soaking the qinghao plant (sweet wormwood) in water and then drinking the liquid.

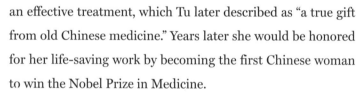

After testing and refining the compound, Tu and her team announced they had found an effective treatment, which Tu later described as "a true gift from old Chinese medicine." Years later she would be honored for her life-saving work by becoming the first Chinese woman to win the Nobel Prize in Medicine.

For Tu Youyou, discovering the solution to a deadly problem required blending old and new knowledge together. This is often described as intersection thinking—the idea that two seemingly unrelated ideas can be combined into something groundbreaking and new. Other times, inspiration can come from the intersection between two unrelated industries.

A more recent example of this is the evolution of the bank-owned café. Workplace surveys have routinely found that the coffee shop vibe is highly rated by office workers, particularly as an antidote to the isolation of remote work. At the same time, despite the sophistication of online banking tools, most people still prefer to get financial advice from a human expert.

{ Examining the intersection of markets and industries might help you spot a non-obvious solution or idea. }

The convergence of these facts has led several large banks to invest in opening more than a hundred bank café locations across the world. These destinations are part bank branch and part coffee shop. These cafés work because they meet people's diverse needs in one physical space where several societal trends intersect: a place for human connection, a space to work remotely, and the chance to get face-to-face advice from a financial expert.

Seeking intersections can help you define a twist in your thinking and lead to a new combined direction that is better than its components.

HOW TO
Mind the Intersections

What Would "They" Do?

In Non-Obvious Thinking workshops, we sometimes challenge participants to solve a problem as if they were working for a different organization. How might someone at NASA approach a problem? How would a data analyst? Or a marketing director? When you need to come up with new solutions to a problem, it can help to imagine how someone in another situation might solve or respond to it. Then find intersections between their methods and yours.

Follow the Trends

When you read about trends, you might be tempted to see them only as descriptions of how individual behavior or broader culture are shifting. While they

describe these changes, they often reveal intersections also. What do two trends from disparate reports or industries have in common? Is there an idea that might be inspired by putting them together? A clever way to use trends is to spark new ideas and intersections through the cultural shifts that the trends describe.

DEFINE THE TWIST

Seek Flip Solutions

Find Option C

Practice Enigmatology

Think Un-Whatever

Mind the Intersections

Create Your Argot

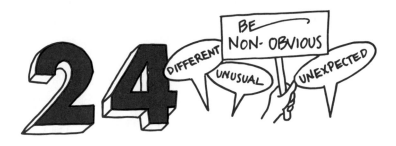

DEFINE THE TWIST //

Create Your Argot

Phil Dusenberry, the former CEO of famed ad agency BBDO, was riding in a taxi the night before presenting a big pitch to General Electric (GE). His team's task was to develop a tagline for the massive brand that would anchor a new global advertising campaign. The best they had come up with was, "We make the things that make life good." It wasn't good enough.

That night, Dusenberry finally came up with something better. The next day for the pitch, his team walked in with their revised tagline: "GE ... We bring good things to life."

GE loved it so much that the slogan would remain in service for decades, not only as the anchor for its ad campaign but also as a rallying cry for employees and a purpose statement for stakeholders. The advertising industry has recognized it with multiple awards as one of the most iconic slogans ever. The right words can shift perceptions. They matter because they can inspire people, or even change how we perceive reality by driving us to believe in something or against something else. This is why politicians and their advisors spend so much time boiling their message down to a handful of words, particularly in an election year.

$$\left\{ \begin{array}{l} \text{The words you use can help your} \\ \text{idea stand out as non-obvious or be} \\ \text{dismissed as stale and obvious.} \end{array} \right\}$$

If you want your ideas to be provocative and memorably non-obvious, the words you choose to describe them make a big difference. The good news is this doesn't require being a world-class ad executive. One way to start doing this for yourself is to think like a linguist.

Words often enter mainstream culture after starting as argot—the jargon or lingo used by a particular group. This term from the French was first used to describe the slang of thieves and rogues but has since been adapted to mean any shared language among members of a subculture. Computer hackers have their own argot, as do high school kids and professional athletes. Listening to and learning about these argots can help you understand a demographic group.

Creating your own argot can be a powerful way to define an idea uniquely. It can help people understand, connect, and form a community around you and your ideas. Legendary musicians have become masters at doing this. Taylor Swift has her Swifties. Beyoncé has the Bey Hive. The Grateful Dead have always had their Deadheads. For each group, the name has become a part of the fans' identities.

This book and our shared philosophy are also examples of the power of an intentional argot. *Non-Obvious* is the word and brand we chose to describe the sort of thinking we want to see more of in the world. It's the reason we wrote this book.

HOW TO
Create Your Argot

Think in Taglines

One way to zero in on what makes your idea unique is to think in taglines, summarizing your concept as succinctly as possible. Using fewer words to communicate something that might otherwise feel complex can lead you to develop an argot that others will find repeatable. Hollywood marketers are masters

at this. For example, the poster for *Jurassic Park* described the film as "an adventure 65 million years in the making." It's the perfect description for one of the best known action adventure films of all time.

Twist Words

Creating your own argot can start by twisting an existing word to convey an original idea. A few years ago, Rohit wrote about people increasingly trust-

ing something flawed rather than something that felt a little too perfect. Buying so-called "ugly" fruits, which are misshapen but still good, or the long-standing popularity of the Leaning Tower of Pisa are both examples of this same principle at work. He called this trend *unperfect* rather than the existing word *imperfect*. This small change communicated the unique nuance of the idea—and made it memorable.

Confidence is belief in yourself.
Certainty is belief in your beliefs.
Confidence is a bridge.
Certainty is a barricade.

—Kevin Ashton
Author of *How to Fly a Horse*

Conclusion

In 2012, a science team on an Australian survey ship headed to a spot 700 miles east of Queensland to visit Sandy Island and made a startling discovery. It wasn't there.

The scientists had arrived exactly where all modern maps and GPS showed the 15-mile-long oval-shaped island to be for well over 100 years. It was even pictured on Google Maps.

Yet in the spot where the island should have been, there was only 1,400 meters of deep water and no land visible for miles. When the missing island was first reported, it created a flurry of speculation and conspiracy theories.

Was this another Atlantis or perhaps a secret military base? Could some cataclysmic event have led to the disappearance of an entire island?

Over time, the most widely accepted explanation turned out to be somewhat less dramatic. The island had never existed in the first place. The fact that it had been included on maps of the time was explained away by a combination of nautical errors and wishful thinking by too-long-at-sea captains that had persisted for generations. Until that fateful long overdue moment when someone thought to confirm there really was an island there and *undiscovered* it.

After confirming the nonexistence of Sandy Island, Google officially removed it from its maps. Others followed. Across the annals of human history, the idea of undiscovery is hardly discussed, but perhaps it should be. While rare, this geographic correction awakened the public's imagination to the tantalizing possibility that perhaps our entire world isn't quite as known as we sometimes think it is.

If an island that was thought to be real for over a century could turn out not to be, what other entrenched mistakes about the way things work remain unknown even today?

{ **Non-obvious thinking often requires questioning the things that we know so we can shift and broaden our perspective.** }

There is a Sandy Island in each of our mental maps. The challenge is discovering (or sometimes undiscovering) what it is and choosing to see the truth.

In Scotland, a recent effort by lexicographers at the University of Glasgow to build a thesaurus of the Scottish language revealed there are over 400 words for snow, including *flindrikin* (a slight snow shower) and *skelf* (a large snowflake).

The interesting thing about being stuck in a Scottish flindrikin, though, is that your experience of the snow doesn't depend on knowing the word for it. No two snowflakes look alike after all ... even if one of them happens to be a skelf.

There will always be things like language or culture or beliefs that offer reasons for seeing the gaps between your experience and others'. But beneath these contrasts, there is more that brings us together if you look deeper.

Opening your mind to see other perspectives takes bravery. Choosing to engage with people unlike yourself or seeking information that is outside your usual media diet does too. More than anything else, this book is about unlocking this sort of mental courage in yourself and using it to see the things that others miss.

That's what non-obvious thinkers do, and the more of us there are in the world, the better the future will be.

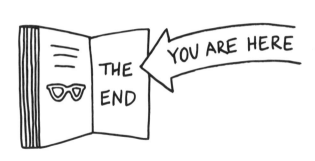

Further Reading

As we came together to write this book, we also turned to our book shelves to pull out the ideas that had inspired us most.

In the following pages, you'll find a curated list of the books that we have found ourselves recommending most over the years. On your journey to become a non-obvious thinker, this reading list is designed to be a guide in continuing to build your skills and knowledge. One of the best ways to do that is to read more books.

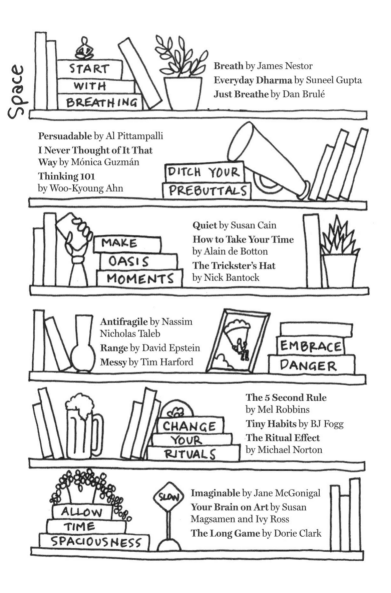

Space

START WITH BREATHING

Breath by James Nestor
Everyday Dharma by Suneel Gupta
Just Breathe by Dan Brulé

Persuadable by Al Pittampalli
I Never Thought of It That Way by Mónica Guzmán
Thinking 101 by Woo-Kyoung Ahn

DITCH YOUR PREBUTTALS

MAKE OASIS MOMENTS

Quiet by Susan Cain
How to Take Your Time by Alain de Botton
The Trickster's Hat by Nick Bantock

Antifragile by Nassim Nicholas Taleb
Range by David Epstein
Messy by Tim Harford

EMBRACE DANGER

CHANGE YOUR RITUALS

The 5 Second Rule by Mel Robbins
Tiny Habits by BJ Fogg
The Ritual Effect by Michael Norton

ALLOW TIME SPACIOUSNESS

SLOW

Imaginable by Jane McGonigal
Your Brain on Art by Susan Magsamen and Ivy Ross
The Long Game by Dorie Clark

Insight

Stop Asking Questions
by Andrew Warner

Talk to Me by Dean Nelson

You're Not Listening
by Kate Murphy

ASK STORY QUESTIONS

What Every Body Is Saying by Joe
Navarro and Marvin Karlins

The Power of Nunchi by Euny Hong

How Work Works
by Michelle P. King

HONE YOUR NUNCHI

Shop Class as Soulcraft
by Matthew B. Crawford

**Why We Make Things and Why
It Matters** by Peter Korn

The Design of Everyday Things
by Don Norman

GET YOUR HANDS DIRTY

What's It Like to Be a Bird?
by David Allen Sibley

Sentient by Jackie Higgins

Nature's Wild Ideas
by Kristy Hamilton

SPOT NATURAL WISDOM

The Art of Gathering
by Priya Parker

Belong by Radha Agrawal

The 2-Hour Cocktail Party
by Nick Gray

FIND THE RIGHT ROOM

STEP INTO OTHERS' SHOES

The Light We Give
by Simran Jeet Singh

Don't Label Me by Irshad Manji

Blindspot by Mahzarin R. Banaji
and Anthony G. Greenwald

FOCUS

The Ministry of Common Sense
by Martin Lindstrom

The Formula
by Albert-László Barabási

Upstream by Dan Heath

IDENTIFY THE REAL PROBLEM

DISCOVER THE WATER

The Trend Forecaster's Handbook
by Martin Raymond

Peak Mind by Amishi P. Jha

Stolen Focus by Johann Hari

BE A SATISFICER

The Paradox of Choice
by Barry Schwartz

Essentialism
by Greg McKeown

The Laws of Simplicity
by John Maeda

Six Thinking Hats
by Edward de Bono

True or False by Cindy Otis

The Sum of Us
by Heather McGhee

SEE THE OTHER SIDE

Subtract by Leidy Klotz

Steal Like an Artist
by Austin Kleon

Digital Minimalism
by Cal Newport

ADD CONSTRAINTS

USE AUGMENTED CREATIVITY

The Artist's Way
by Julia Cameron

How to Fly a Horse
by Kevin Ashton

The Back of the Napkin
by Dan Roam

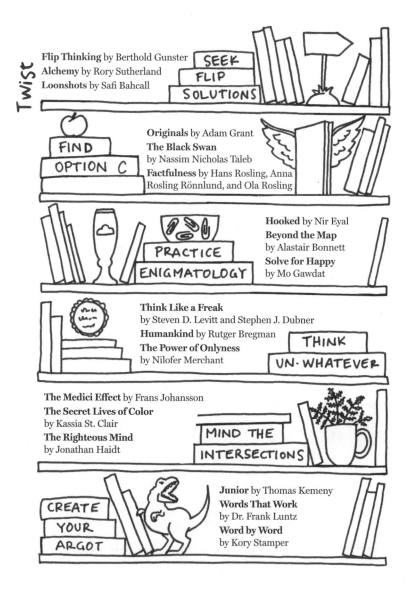

Twist

Flip Thinking by Berthold Gunster
Alchemy by Rory Sutherland
Loonshots by Safi Bahcall

SEEK
FLIP
SOLUTIONS

FIND
OPTION C

Originals by Adam Grant
The Black Swan
by Nassim Nicholas Taleb
Factfulness by Hans Rosling, Anna
Rosling Rönnlund, and Ola Rosling

PRACTICE
ENIGMATOLOGY

Hooked by Nir Eyal
Beyond the Map
by Alastair Bonnett
Solve for Happy
by Mo Gawdat

Think Like a Freak
by Steven D. Levitt and Stephen J. Dubner
Humankind by Rutger Bregman
The Power of Onlyness
by Nilofer Merchant

THINK
UN·WHATEVER

The Medici Effect by Frans Johansson
The Secret Lives of Color
by Kassia St. Clair
The Righteous Mind
by Jonathan Haidt

MIND THE
INTERSECTIONS

CREATE
YOUR
ARGOT

Junior by Thomas Kemeny
Words That Work
by Dr. Frank Luntz
Word by Word
by Kory Stamper

Non-Obvious Endnotes

This is a book filled with stories. Sometimes, you may find yourself intrigued enough to want to read more about one of them. Rather than follow the usual high school bibliography format you'll often find in books, we wanted to create some endnotes to satisfy the most curious among you. In this section, you'll find some context around each story we used along with a place you can go to keep reading and learning more.

Non-Obvious Thinkers ask questions, and if this book sparked some new ones for you ... we hope this section will help you find a few answers!

2   **Fosbury Flop**: For a good overview of this story, watch a video from the official Olympics YouTube channel here: https://youtu.be/CZsH46Ek2ao.

14   **most influential books of the past decade**: Near the end of 2019 as a new decade was about to begin, CNN compiled a list of the top ten most influential books of the past ten years. See the full list here: https://www.cnn.com/2019/12/30/entertainment/decades-most-influential-books-trnd/index.html.

20   **"there are as many ways to breathe as there are foods to eat"**: James Nestor, *Breath: The New Science of a Lost Art* (Riverhead Books, 2020), pg. xvi, Introduction.

33   **one key difference between introverts and extroverts**: Susan Cain, *Quiet: The Power of Introverts in a World That Can't Stop Talking* (Crown, 2012).

38   **interesting theory to explain this paradox**: The story of The Land was told in a documentary film referenced in the chapter as well as several articles online. A good starting point for this story is an article published in *The Atlantic* magazine from April 2014 titled "The Overprotected Kid." Read the full article here: https://www.theatlantic.com/magazine/archive/2014/04/hey-parents-leave-those-kids-alone/358631/.

39   **habitual use of GPS has negatively affected our spatial memory**: This study from Louisa Dahmani and Véronique D. Bohbot, published in 2017, was titled "Habitual Use of GPS Negatively Impacts Spatial Memory during Self-Guided Navigation" and outlined the negative effects on our spatial memory from overreliance on GPS. Read the original study here: https://doi.org/10.1038/s41598-020-62877-0.

45   **chai instead of coffee**: *Chai* is the Hindi word for "tea," so the widely misused phrase "chai tea" is unnecessarily repetitive and incorrect.

45   **a different fruit every morning for a month**: *TIME*, May 22, 2014. "10 Questions with Ferran Adrià." https://time.com/108688/10-questions-with-ferran-adria/.

46   **"poem of the day"**: Read the poem of the day from *Poetry* magazine at https://www.poetryfoundation.org/poems/poem-of-the-day.

47   **consider self-help guru Mel Robbins's advice**: Mel Robbins, *The 5 Second Rule: Transform Your Life, Work, and Confidence with Everyday Courage* (Savio Republic, 2017).

50   **earn well over $10 billion dollars**: Box office projections cited in the book for James Cameron's films were sourced from the industry website Screenrant.com: https://screenrant.com/james-cameron-highest-grossing-director-avatar-prediction-when/.

51   **"the relaxing and empowering feeling that we have enough time to do what really matters"**: Jane McGonigal, *Imaginable: How to See the Future Coming and Feel Ready for Anything—Even Things That Seem Impossible Today* (Spiegel & Grau, 2022), pg. 8.

57   **"you are more beautiful than you think"**: A month after the Dove Real Beauty Sketches ad first aired in 2013, it had more than 50 million views and went on to be one of the most shared videos that year. For more context on the campaign and to watch the original video, see https://www.dove.com/us/en/stories/campaigns/real-beauty-sketches.html.

61   **inspired aspiring journalists for decades with her methods**: These storytelling methods were outlined by Lauren Klinger in a 2015 article for journalism non-profit The Poynter Institute titled "'Don't Be Boring' and 6 Other Interviewing

Tips From Jacqui Banaszynski." Read the article here: https://www.poynter.org/ newsletters/2015/dont-be-boring-and-6-other-interviewing-tips-from-jacqui-banaszynski/.

67   *nunchi*: Read more about how to practice nunchi in *The Power of Nunchi: The Korean Secret to Happiness and Success* by Euny Hong, first published by Penguin Life in 2019.

67   *kuuki wo yomu*: While there are several good articles you might translate from Japanese explaining this concept, a good English language description comes from this BBC article: https://www.bbc.com/worklife/article/20200129-what-is-reading-the-air-in-japan.

70   **turning point in the election**: For further analysis of the Nixon-Kennedy debate and the role body language played in voters' perceptions, this article from the National Constitution Center is a good resource: https://constitutioncenter.org/blog/the-debate-that-changed-the-world-of-politics.

73   *Why we suck*: Read more about this meeting and what happened next in this article: https://fortune.com/2023/09/07/uber-ceo-drive-deliver-why-we-suck/.

79   **termite mounds**: The way termite mounds are formed is a fascinating example of nature at work. Read more about how they get their shape here: https://seas.harvard.edu/news/2019/02/how-termite-mounds-get-their-shape.

79   **self-ventilating building**: The full story behind this building, including research downloads, is available from the architect Mick Pearce's website at https://www.mickpearce.com/Eastgate.html.

80   **biomimicry**: For more examples of human innovations that have been inspired by nature, here's a good recap: https://cosmosmagazine.com/technology/10-technologies-inspired-by-nature/.

85   **a small group of scientists and thinkers huddled inside a room:** In 2012, *WIRED* magazine assembled a dozen of the confirmed participants of this meeting together and published a candid interview with them about what they recalled from the "idea summit" (as it was later called). Read the article here: https://www.wired.com/2012/06/minority-report-idea-summit/.

92   **"empathy engine"**: This term is now used widely to describe the potential of virtual reality technology. It is most popularly credited to immersive storyteller Chris Milk, who used the term in his TED Talk from 2015. Watch the talk here: https://www.ted.com/talks/chris_milk_how_virtual_reality_can_create_the_ultimate_empathy_machine.

95   **weak ties**: This term is based on the concept of "weak tie theory"—an idea first introduced by sociologist Mark Granovetter in his 1973 paper "The Strength of Weak Ties." The theory argues that in some situations, such as discovering new ideas or finding your next job, acquaintances outside your usual social circle can be far more helpful than your inner circle of close friends and family. Multiple research studies over the past 50 years since this theory was first published have confirmed this same conclusion.

98   **Damascus rose oil**: For a deeper look at the story of how Turkish farmers harvest rose oil, the Stories + Objects website features an interview with a rose harvester in Isparta, Turkey, named Esengül Artisoy about her daily routine during harvest season. Full story here: https://www.storiesandobjects.com/blogs/stories/a-turkish-rose.

99 **Waterford crystal apprenticeship**: The best description of this eight-year-long apprenticeship can be found on the Waterford website, along with images of the famous Waterford bowl completed by all apprentices: https://www.waterford.com/en-us/discover-waterford/the-waterford-story/craftsmanship.

104 **"fifty inventions that shaped the modern economy"**: The story of Otis and his appearance at the 1853 World's Fair has been told many times on the internet and in various publications. The story also appears in Chapter 22 of Tim Harford's excellent book *Fifty Inventions That Shaped the Modern Economy,* published by Riverhead Books in 2017.

106 **frustrated by a $40 fee from Blockbuster**: There is some debate online about whether this story is true. Netflix co-founder Marc Randolph has said it was fiction, and Hastings himself has been elusive about this. It's likely that he did experience frustration at getting a late fee (quite common for anyone who is old enough to remember Blockbuster!), and we believed this was one among many factors that inspired the Netflix business model, so we chose to keep the story in this book. Read more here: https://www.cnbc.com/2017/05/23/netflix-ceo-reed-hastings-on-how-the-company-was-born.html.

107 **five whys method**: This method was born in the world of manufacturing and is still cited by many groups, including the American Society of Quality, as a viable technique for identifying and solving process problems. Read an overview here: https://asq.org/quality-resources/five-whys.

109 **"Goldilocks zone"**: Also known as the "habitable zone," this theory was first introduced by Chinese-born American astrophysicist Su-Shu Huang in 1959. Read more about his theories here: https://www.scientificamerican.com/article/life-outside-the-solar-system/.

115 **most people are *maximizers* or *satisficers***: The quotes in this chapter are taken from *The Paradox of Choice* by Barry Schwartz (Ecco, 2004).

121 **duck or rabbit image**: This image is legendary among both philosophers and psychologists and has been used in countless experiments over the past century since it was first published. There are multiple versions of this image drawn by various artists, and it has most often been used to demonstrate what philosophers call "aspect perception"—the concept that the same thing can be viewed from different perspectives.

122 **around Easter time, more people were likely to see the rabbit:** For more details about this study and others that have been done using this image, read this article: https://www.independent.co.uk/news/science/duck-and-rabbit-illusion-b1821663.html.

123 **Magic Eye book series**: In 1991, engineer Tom Baccei and 3D artist Cheri Smith collaborated with programmer Bob Salitsky to create the first Magic Eye® 3D Illusions. The images become a worldwide craze in the early '90s and inspired a *New York Times* bestselling series of books. An infrequently updated website about the series history is still available online at https://www.magiceye.com/about/.

128 **"that first graders can't put down"**: The story of Dr. Seuss rising to the challenge of writing stories with a limited word count is retold in a profile of the author on Biography.com. Read the full article here: https://www.biography.com/authors-writers/dr-seuss-green-eggs-and-ham-bet.